Johann Isaac HOLLANDUS

De Lapide Philosophorum

Prologue

To the Book by Johannes Isaac Hollandus on the Philosophers' Stone

In this prologue you will be taught of what kind of work everybody should be aware.

My child, you must know that in this Art there are many mistakes, especially in the Vegetable Work. The reason for this is the following: In the Vegetable Work there is much coagulating, dissolving, and rectifying to well prepare the spirits so that they do not fly away; also much aquafort has to be made and many watery spirits fixed. It requires much regulating of the fire and much concern lest the spirits break the vessels, for their fat moisture often causes the glasses to burst if they are given too strong a fire when they are about to become fixed. Then they rise and stay locked within the glass, and in rising (expanding) they break the glass. Then, all one's labor is lost, and, therefore, one has to be on guard. This then is the great worry, as you well now if you have attempted to do some work, In addition, much work and time are required for the rectification of the wine; also, much work to make the Water fixed and to keep the spirits from flying away. All that requires a long time, as is known by all who have tried it. Further, much work and time are required for the putrefaction and digestion, which have to be handled very delicately with the proper regimen, not too weak and not too strong. Also, one has to be cautious at all times to keep the regimen (of fire) with great care, as many are already well aware.

There is still another problem. That is, to calcine and improve the Bodies and the Earth in such a way that they are not burnt in the glass or become dry. Therefore, one has to take special care to maintain a good regimen of the Fire and to work with great caution.

Furthermore, the Earth must be calcined and clarified, then the Water again distilled, as so forth with all the operations that are a part of this work.

Moreover, in the composition, one must not take too much of one and too little of the other, because, if you have well preserved your fatness in the beginning, the medicine has no ingress, then you will have worries with your work and the possibility of it being spoiled. Thus, there is much danger, great expense, and if we believe that we have done everything right and that nothing is lacking in the prescribed process, we may yet have been careless and kept the fire too hot or not hot enough, through negligence. If we now wish to make a projection with our work and it does not do what we intended it to do, and we therefore do not obtain any benefit from it, and we do not know what may be wrong or how it could have happened, it is still the non-observance of the details of the prescribed manipulation which we have here related.

Therefore, I advise you, my children, not to undertake the Vegetablili Opus for the above mentioned reasons, because a small error might spoil your work and then all you have invested in time and money is lost. This is why I advise you to be very careful with the Vegetable Work, because of the separation of the elements, the separation and rectification required in it, also on account of the serious worries you will have for a long time and the many kinds of uncertainty which may occur. The work takes a long time and it is difficult to see the end.

If you lose the natural moisture at the beginning, your work will become too dry in its composition; or if it loses some Spirit of Air in the distillation due to a faulty vessel or leak in the luting, you will lose your high projection. If you lose some in the Fire, your medicine will not tincture much and will also lose its ability to ingress. If it has too much Air, it will fly away, if it has too much Water, the Spirits will drown so that it cannot be fixed, If it has too much Earth, it will be to dry, so that it can neither melt no have ingress. Therefore the work of the separation of the Elements involves a great deal of concerns, as many mistakes can occur.

Likewise in the rectification, and if anything in the Elements is spoiled, no matter how little, the whole work is spoiled! That is why I advise you, dear Sons who are afraid of all operations in which the Elements have to be separated, be it in the Animal, Mineral, or Vegetable Works, or in the Stone which god has given us for nothing: When the preparation of the Stone has reached the stage of the separation, be afraid for your work because of the uncertainty connected with it. For, it can easily happen that in the beginning and in the middle, some of its moisture can be lost and then the whole work is lost. Because if one tries to put it together, it cannot be combined, and its ingress has also been taken from it. In such a case, your time and expense and labor have been wasted.

There have been masters (the ancient ones) who have done this work, but they only did it in order to understand nature as they had done the great Work before and thus did not have to worry about the cost or labor. Further no great amount of investigation (research) was necessary. We shall discuss this Great Work later, if it be the will of God.

There have also been other artists and philosophers who worked toward miraculous amalgamations, fixations, multiplications and many other marvelous operations which they called 'short works' of one month, or perhaps 8-10 weeks, but which take so long they do not know how to conclude them on account of the mishaps that occur in the work. For they do not preserve their natural moisture at the beginning or the middle of the work, so that it becomes quire dry; or they cook it too hard or too cold or too long on the fire, with the result that it loses its ingress and ability to melt.

Therefore, avoid all amalgamations, multiplications and fixations because, while you may believe that they will go very fast, they will actually take a very long time and thus involve so much concern and labor that you will scarce be able to see the end. In addition, there is the uncertainty connected with the required washing and purification, for no fixation can be made before the Spirit and the Body have been cleaned of all their faeces. However, no fixation or new ingress can occur, even after the washing, cleaning and dissolution, if you lose the Spirit's moisture ~ then all is lost.

Consequently I advise you to avoid all operations requiring washing and cleaning because of the worries, burden, time and expense pertaining to them. Likewise, of a separation of the Elements is to be done, or a distillation, calcinations or coagulation, due to the possible dangers of which I have previously spoken, avoid such operations. Consider that if just one mishap occurs as mentioned above ~ and there are thousands I have nor mentioned since the recounting would take much time to relate — all your expense and time would be lost. This would cause you to become impatient or be discouraged.

Therefore, stay with the Great Art, or the great Elixir, as your foregathers did. When you have accomplished that, you may try other operations of Nature with greater confidence. But if you do otherwise, you are not following my advice. To begin with, take in hand the Great Work, because there is no worry in it. Nothing in it is distilled, dissolved, coagulated or purified. In it there are no unknown works or things, no impure things that hav e faces. Nor do you calcine as there is no need for it. You do not separate any Elements, because they are pure. It is one species, one thing, one vessel, one furnace, and one work — to the White and to the Red.

Therefore, no danger will befall this work. It is nothing but a woman's work and merely child's play. Ignorant men cannot understand this simply because this work is so easy. This because the Great Work dissolves, purifies, coagulates, sublimates, and congeals itself! It also makes itself easy to melt, just like wax, and perfects itself into that which it is supposed to become.

Now, dear Sons, I have shown you many of the accidents that may occur in your work, and you may encounter thousands more of them, about which I will not write for the sake of brevity. Be wise, therefore, so that you are not ruined if you should meet with any of them. I told you so before, in plain words and without any parables. If I were to write to you about Sebbal, Carabric, Marmeth, Sebbaim, Mirrath, Alleb and Raphirib, etc., etc., how difficult it would be for you to understand! But I have now revealed this matter to your mind and to your understanding, so that you should not fail in this regard.

Therefore, I recommend the great Work to you, for in it there is no failure, worry, work or vigil. Nor can it be spoiled, unless it be done deliberately. You need no foreign spirits, or conjuring, or a multitude of glasses, you only need one vessel and no more, one species of matter and no more, one oven and no more. That is why Geber says: Our Stone is one species, one thing. Therefore ignorant men cannot understand it. No foreign things that are not of its nature are added to our Stone. Ignorant men wish to bring it into its nature because they are unable to congeal this one thing. But when they do succeed in congealing it, they are right back to where they started from. Then it is nothing but earth that has lost its moisture. It cannot flow and it has no ingress. This is true because they stop when they should actually start (the work). Now, if they knew of what species this subject is and recognized its father and mother, sister and brother, arm in arm, mouth to mouth, they would die at once! If they would recognize and understand these things, they would obtain all their desires from the Art, and all their works would end happily.

Dear Sons, I have revealed all this to you in clear words. Therefore, do not undertake anything with unknown operations before you have accomplished the Opus Magnum. Following that, start whatever you wish and do not spare any expense or time because you will have as much of both these as you want. I have mentioned the many accidents that may occur, and there are many others as well. But you should know that there exists an easy rule of which the Philosophers all speak of in a strange way, using parables and expounding it under veiled names, and yet, they are all referring to the great Work. Those who are able to perform the Great Work can also understand all the parables and the veiled words. In addition, you should understand and know about this work that the true Art is in al things, and it is true! You are to understand it as follows: Every determined thing contains its perfect medicine, though it is in an unprepared form. If you know how to prepare it, you neither need to buy or to have any other medicines. All this needs to be understood.

No disease in the world can come upon a man because he has the perfect remedy within himself whereby he can completely recover. That is, providing he knows how to prepare it properly. He can obtain it from himself and prepare it so it will not harm his body. The same applies to all animals, birds, plants and anything created by God. It is indeed so, but ignorant men cannot understand what the old sages said and they think they can make a medicine from all things. That is why they take eggs, blood, urine and the like, believing that they can thereby bring into perfection, imperfect bodies. And when they have done, they are still at the start and remain immersed in their stupidity.

But my child should know that a man generates a man. A horse generates a horse, a bird a bird, each its like, otherwise it would be contrary to Nature. This is the reason that metal cannot be made from such sperm as blood and eggs. Where there is nothing, do not try to extract anything from an imperfect thing. To transmute metals into Sol and Luna from such is against Nature and reason. Clearly it is not possible. It is a wonder that some should have seized upon such a fantasy. If they understood the workings of Nature, they would never have made such a mistake.

Know that all oils of metals re elixirs, likewise all salts, It is also known that all imperfect metals contain within them their medicine. How much better will be the oil of Sol or Luna as both are perfect.

Dear Sons, you should know that a perfect medicine can be made from all metals, which can transmute all imperfect metals into gold and silver without separation of the elements, also without distilling, sublimating, dissolving or fixing. It dissolves itself and purifies itself, it coagulates itself, distills, sublimates, congeals and calcines itself! It can also cause itself to melt and flow. Furthermore, it is also possible to extract oils from all metals in different ways. Likewise, salt can be extracted from all metals without separation of the Elements, and this concerns the Great Work!

De Lapide Philosophorum

by

Johannes Isaac Hollandus

Here Begins the Work of the Ancients with Perfect Instruction,
With Nothing Being Omitted from This

Now, dear Sons, we shall write about the Magnum opus (Great Work) which our forefathers used in many different ways. They all reached their goal, but their Stone did not make the same projection, but one made a higher than the other after they had made the work subtle. After that, they also obtained high colors. The ancients worked long before they produced the Stone. With subtlety, they shortened the work, just as it is being done today. Understand, our parents required three or four years before they could perfect the Stone. This was because at that time, they knew no strong water, only distilled vinegar. Now, their descendants have invented aquafort (AF); which has greatly shortened the work. You should know that the work can be shortened even more through the first labor, in as much as one must make the metals subtle and mingled, so that it turns into a dough-like matter. That is why Hermes Philosophus says: Do not be lazy at the beginning of your work; cleanse your subject well and clearly, and conjoin it subtly, so that you can rejoice afterwards. Geber, Dandin and Morienus also say: Unite well the water with the earth and the moist with the dry so that you see later the blackness of the sea, that is, its black color, which you should see during putrefaction, which is to occur in 24 days, with a gentle fire. It is a favorable sign of good union.

Therefore, my child, be diligent in the beginning, so that you prepare your material carefully and well; for as soon as it is put in the fire, you have already done all your work and must not be concerned about anything but the regulation of the fire. You must know that I intend to relate afterwards, many operations, which are always perfect.

First, our parents worked towards amalgamations, with Sol and Luna, which is a very perfect work, yet rather long. However, it is also the most surest and the one with the least worries. They also undertook amalgamation in a variety of ways. Nonetheless, they all reached their goal, though not with the same height of projection. Further, some among them shortened the work more than others through subtlety, as we will teach in the Vegetable Work.

The Work of the Old Masters

Know, dear Sons, that there were some old alchemists who took fine silver, well refined in the crucible and filed as subtly as possible, 3 Lots, and fine old cemented through the cement regale, 1 Lot; well purified Mercury, 8 Lots. They amalgamated all this well in an iron mortar with a steel pestle, grinding it for 12 or 14 hours. After this, they put it in a stone or glass vessel, formed as illustrated (a round-bottom Florence flask), set it in sand so hot that one could not keep one's finger in it, and they let it stand thus to allow the moisture to evaporate. In the morning they found that the matter was hard. Again they put it in the mortar, added yet half a part of Mercury, or 4 Lots, to make the inner parts even. They continued with this manual labor till the matter could be pressed dry though a double linen cloth. Thereafter, they set it for another 8 days in the sand with its vessel, and pounded the matter in the mortar every day for 8 hours without stopping.

When the 8 days are over, take the matter and put it in a glass as illustrated (Florence flask), press on the opening a piece of cut glass that closes it tightly, add a weight and set it in tripodem, and heat it so much that you can keep you hand between the walls of the furnace and the glass which contains the matter. Thus they kept the fire going day and night for six weeks, and at the end of the six weeks they increased it a little, as if to keep lead in fusion. They maintained this heat until they saw perfect blackness. Then they rejoiced, as under the blackness is hidden the whiteness, and it is a sure sign that the matter has been well conjoined at the beginning. Remember also that you must lift the over from the furnace on the third day and see of some drops of Mercury adhere to the glass above. You must shake them down, and if they do not fall down, remove the glass and brush them down with a feather to make them drop down again on the matter. Now stopper the glass again, and do this each time on the third and fourth day.

It is so much better to give only a little heat, to prevent the matter from rising. It will take more time, but that does not matter. It is better to have a sure result than an uncertain one, as you might spoil your Work with too much heat. Watch out, too, that you do not get the red color before the white one, because one color changes into another. These are also many foreign colors, but you must not heed them. Pay attention only to the three colors, which must appear in the Work: First, the blackness, then the whiteness, and finally the redness. Between these three colors there will appear many colors, more than one can imagine, but do not pay attention to them. They are flying spirits which are not yet fixed, and they are poisonous. As long as you see the foreign spirits, beware of the air, as it might kill you. The first red colors that show up appear with a gentle regimen of the fire, or if the fire is increased only a little.

In this Art there is no worry except how to regulate the Fire. But if you wish to be very sure, keep your fire as small as possible. Then you cannot go wrong, although it takes somewhat more time. Therefore I advise and teach you, dear Sons, not to heat too strongly, so that you do not get the red color before the white one, because this same red color, if it appeared before the white, would look in the glass like pulverized bricks, like grains of wheat or barley, or larger, with intermixed grains of live Mercury, and it would attack the glass. Then all your Work would be spoiled. If this does happen, it is solely due to the too strong fire. The right color, however, does not look like bricks but is a clear dark and brown-red. It is more a heavenly color than a red one,

14

and is due to a good regimen of the fire, as will be taught later. I am telling you of these colors so that you do not fall into error because of ignorance, and do not know what to do or what to omit.

Now We Will Proceed Further With Our Work

If with a small fire something rises in the neck of the glass or on the cover, open the glass and push it back to the bottom, as I have told you. Keep it standing thus day and night till your matter becomes completely pulverized. The powder should be grey and black, like earth that has lost its moisture. Before you come to this color, you will see various strange things, because the matter will become motley and speckled, which all the painters and goldsmiths cannot counterfeit. As the matter becomes riper and stronger, a change occurs, and before you reach the grey-black powder, your matter will become a lovely yellowish, like wood, or peat ash. All this happens with a low regimen of the fire for a long time and watch whether your matter retains this color or whether it becomes whiter and brighter. Of it becomes whiter or paler, keep the same regimen of the fire. But if the color is such that you can neither see nor sense that it changes somewhat, increase the fire a little till you notice the color becoming paler or whiter. Then let it stand for a long time in the same regimen of the fire, always taking care not to make it too strong, till your matter is white, yea, whiter than snow. Then be glad, dear children, and be sure that under the whiteness the beautiful redness lies hidden.

Morienus says: When Christ lay in the tomb, a resurrection was to take place, and after that resurrection a glorious Body shall live in all eternity, and be crowned with a red diadem, and shall be king over all his line, and all his enemies shall make peace with him, and he shall remain king for ever and ever.

You must understand that this white matter or earth is nothing but an earth that has lost its moisture and is still of

16

no use. That is why you must know that there are many mistakes in this Art, for there are many who dare to make the Philosophers' Stone, and indeed reach this degree with a good regimen of the fire, and endeavor to fix this Stone to the White or the Red. When this matter or Stone is fixed, they believe that they can make projection by throwing it on raw Mercury or other imperfect metals — but to no avail. Then they become despondent and say that the Art is impossible. True, it is impossible for them, because their earth has lost its moisture, just as Geber says: Spirits which have lost their moisture due to many sublimations and fixation are useless as long as they are earth and therefore dry like the latter. The ignorant do not understand this, and after they have made their Stone and it has the right color, it must again be made subtile and volatile if it is to have ingress and make projection. However, they do not understand the words of the wise. They may well know how to make the Stone and do indeed make it as it is supposed to be made, but they abandon the Work just when they should begin to labour properly, and thus they remain in their foolish error.

You must know, dear Sons, that I wish to reveal here the real secret of the Art. Therefore I beseech you, by the living God, not to disclose the secret except to your own Sons, provided you believe that they have the love of God and that your soul, and also mine, will not be damned because of it, as great troubles might result. Open your eyes and ears, see and hear the great sacredness in nature, namely, that all Philosophers' Stones, no matter how they are composed, can be made and completed in the Great Work of which we are here speaking, both to the White and to the Red, in one vessel and one furnace.

Remember well what I am telling you: If you combine Luna and mercury with Sol in this manner, you can make the Stone from them, either to the White or to the Red, in one vessel and in one furnace.

Now someone might ask: Why then must Luna and Sol be taken together in this Work?

The reason is that Sol is fixed, and therefore the Work will be the shorter for it. If your Luna were fixed in the Work, the Philosophers Stone would be ready. But it is not fixed, and before it becomes fixed, much time and cooking are required, as Luna must be fixed before it congeals Mercury. This is the reason why Luna and Sol are used together in the Work. You can also make both Stones with Mercury and Sol alone, and that would take les time than with Luna and Sol together, the reason being that Sol is fixed and that therefore it congeals Mercury somewhat.

Someone might ask: If one were to take only Luna and Mercury together, what would be the result? Could the red Stone also be prepared from them?

This is to be understood as follows: Luna is red in its innermost just as it is white outside, for under all white things that contain the four Elements, there is a redness inside, covered with the white on the outside. Luna is cold and moist, just as Mercury and Luna coagulated together. They are still raw and unfixed, and that is why they are white outside and red inside.

When Luna is alone in the Work with Mercury, it has to be completely cooked and congealed with a good regimen of the fire. When it has become fixed, it congeals the Mercury and becomes a white Philosophers' Stone. By increasing the fire and cooking it for a long time, the white Stone is colored red, its tincture comes out and the whiteness goes inside.

Consider well, dear children, what I have said and still have to say. It is absolutely necessary, for it is the secret of all works. There have been some ignorant men who after making their Stone to the White and the Red, saw that it had no ingress and did not flow like wax. Seeing that the ingress was lacking, they dissolved the Stone, coagulated it again 20 or 30 times, hoping to make the Stone fusible in this Way, so as to give it ingress. They did not succeed, and even if they were to dissolve and coagulate till Doomsday, their Stone would remain as it had been before.

There have been others who extracted an oil from Antimony. With that they pounded the Stone on marble, dried it again in a glass, imbibed it so long and so much that the Stone became liquid like wax and had an ingress. Then they threw it on red-hot Mercury, and as soon as the Mercury glowed, it flew away and the oil followed it. The powder of the Stone was left behind in the crucible just as it had been before they imbibed it. This was due to the fact that the oil had not yet been fixed, and although the Stone was liquid, the oil was not congealed with the Stone. The reason is: If the Stone were then thus imbibed and put in a glass with a gentle heat, the oil would become dry with the Stone. If it were given a strong fire, however, the oil would fly away altogether from the great heat. That is why the oil cannot be congealed together with the Stone. Thus the ignorant have remained in their error.

Now I will teach you, my child, how to make the Stone fusible and to give it ingress, which has never before been revealed. Therefore, dear Sons, keep the secret to yourselves, if you love God, your soul and mine,

After your Stone has become white by means of good regimen of the fire, as I taught you before, you can keep it white, if you like. But if you want it to become red, you must let it stand much longer in the furnace, increasing the fire considerably. When you see that it begins to become yellow like mastic, do not make the fire stronger. Let it stand thus in great heat or 8 or 9 days, and look if the Stone has become somewhat more yellow. If it is the same color, increase the fire considerably, and if it begins to take on the color of saffron (crocus) let it stand in the same regimen for 8 or 9 days.

Proceed thus continually with the regimen of fire till you see the perfect redness, like a glowing old in the fire, and it appears to be more a heavenly color than an earthly one.

Thus the Stone must be cooked with a strong fire, as a small fire does not cause its tincture and sulphur ~ that is, its red tincture ~ to come forth. And before it obtains its perfect redness, it must stand for 41 days.

Know that if the Stone were liquid, its redness could not be brought out because it would melt in becoming red-hot and even penetrate through the glass and thus be lost, since it must finally glow for 3 days. Concerning this, you have to take not that the Stone must first be made before it is made fusible. This the ignorant cannot understand or remember, because they do not know Nature. Therefore, both the white and the red Stones must be made before they are made fusible and subtle, as you yourselves may understand.

Now, Hear My Sons, the Greatest Secret ~

That lies in the Art and which has never been put in writing except now by myself, how to prepare and melt the two Stones, so as to make a high projection with them.

Take your Stone and imbibe it with clean Paradise Water. Unite it with the water, imprison it, and close tightly. It will rise to heaven in one cycle of the moon, will be converted into dew and come down again in drops, in accordance with the teaching of the master. It will moisten the earth that it may bring forth flowers of varied colors. At the appearance of those flowers, your Stone will rise from the dead and take on a new body, and all its enemies shall make peace with it, and the storm that was before shall be over. It has overcome the darkness and the eclipse of the Sun and the Moon, and shall forthwith be a king over its species, and shall not lose its dominion in all eternity but shall remain the King of Glory.

Take the Stone, white or red, from the cask in a stone mortar, imbibe it with a good amount of purified Mercury, which I have taught you to prepare. Pound them together with a wooden pestle without stopping for a whole day. After that, put it back in its glass, set it again in the philosophers' stove or in tripodem, and give it as much fire as is used to keep Saturn melting. Seal the glass's mouth and keep it in this heat till all the Mercury is dead. It will take place in 40 or 50 days, because the Stone draws its spirit into its nature, for each seeks its like, and all rejoice in their likes.

When Mercury is dead, raise your fire somewhat till the matter is white. When it is a white Stone, remove it. Make a copper plate red-hot, put on it one grain of the Stone and

21

see if the Stone is liquid and has ingress, so that it can tinge the laminae and go through them like oil through dry leather, turning the plate white like fine silver. If it does so, it is ready. If not, imbibe it again with clean Paradise Water, in due form, as has been taught before. To one ounce of the Stone take 4 Lots of Paradise Water as has been taught before. To 1 ounce of the Stone take 4 Lots of Paradise Water each time you pour the Paradise Water on. Continue doing this till the Stone is liquid and has the ingress you wish. If it is the red Stone, after you have imbibed it with Paradise Water, keep it standing in as much heat as is required to keep lead in fusion till it becomes red again. It will take much longer than with the white Stone. Test it also just like the white Stone.

But this you have to take note of: If you wish to prepare the Stone in order to make projection with it on mercury, it must be made as fusible as wax, and that must be done carefully as the Stone is apt to go through the glass. My advice is that you should make it flow so much that it becomes red-hot before melting. This concerns the white Stone. After this, make projection with it on tin. The red Stone, however, must not be made more liquid. It must well glow but without blazing, for as the Paradise Water it contains is dead and fixed, it must stay in the furnace and glow for 40 days before it comes out red. When the redness is outside, you must raise the fire to keep the Stone glowing constantly. Just enough that you can see it glow, and no more. Let it stand thus for three days, then let it cool, and thank God that your Stone is accomplished.

Dear Sons, You must keep to your measures in all your works and especially when making the Stone fusible, for if you make it too liquid, it will go through the glass, as has been taught before. You must make the red Stone even less liquid or you will be unable to infuse it with the tincture of the Paradise Water. You should know that all things in the world can be made malleable and fusible with the Paradise Water if it is sublimated with tem or pressed into them to make it stay with them. This is called ceratio, and ceratio is nothing but making hard non-fusible things fusible so that they may have ingress. It was first discovered by the old masters. For after seeking a long tie how to make the Stone to the White and the Red, they found that their work was useless as their Stone did not melt and remained as a powder or earth. Then they realized that they were lacking noting but ceratio, which would give ingress. They looked in many and varied things, yet found it in none except sulphur and auripigment, and especially in mercury.

You should also know that the oil of all things in the world separates from its earth in the fire, except that of minerals and metals, because their oil says with the earth in the fire and does not separate from it. If it does separate, the earth rises together with it, as their oils cannot be separated from the earth, which can be done with other things. They knew well that if they wished to follow Nature, they needed such oils to increate and make their spirit and dry earth liquid. They found them in sulphur and auripigment, but ten times more in Mercury.

In this way the art of creation was invented. They made their Stone liquid as they wished, and it did what they desired of their Art. By it they made fusible whatever they wished, they sublimated the spirits through hot things and made them strong and poisonous, so that they became so subtle that it was astonishing. When they had made them thus subtle by subliming and not with corrosive things, and they had absorbed enough of the tinctures, they increated the substance with well purified Mercury, that is, they poured a large quantity of Mercury over it, put it in tripodem, let it ascend and descend until the Mercury stayed with it. Thus they made their spirits fusible as they pleased. They also took Sol and Luna, made into a very subtle calx, imbibed it with purified Mercury and set it in tripodem, in a glass as illustrated. They reversed (turned over) it often and sublimated it till the mercury stayed with it. Thus they made the calx fusible and could tinge with it, namely, they dissolved the calx in vinegar, turned it into subtle crystalline stones which they cleaned carefully, ground them into a powder, imbibed that with fresh Mercury, set it in tripodem, as has been reported about Sol and Luna, and in this way they also made a medicine.

I am telling you, dear Sons, the whole Art lies in creation. Therefore read this over frequently, for it contains great wonders. Consequently, you will be able to make medicines from all metals, as we have taught and said, in a short time, without special effort, harm, or expense, and all with this Art, with the Philosophical Mercury.

Another Work of the Old Masters

There have also been some others who took 3 Lots Silver and 1 Lot Gold. They melted and filed them together, then put the matter into an iron mortar and powdered it fine, so that it could be pressed through a cloth. After that, they rubbed it till it became intangible. Others added to it honey or gum and rubbed it intangibly. They put this into a glass, poured clean water on it, boiled it for one hour, let it stand, then poured it off. Again they poured more water on it, boiled it, let it stand, and poured it off. They did this till the powder was quite pure and no more blackness came out of it. Then they dried the powder, took Mercury pressed though 5 or 6 times and washed perfectly clean with salt and vinegar, put it into a glass, added an alembic, set it in ash with a gentle fire of the kind used to burn roses. They let it stand in this heat for 10 or 12 days, so as to draw its superfluous moisture off, which would harm the Work. This is how every Mercury to be used in the Art must be prepared, but it must not be heated too much lest the mercury sublimate ~ unless it would sublimate only a little. That would not harm it, but if it would rise too much, you must revivify it with warm water, adding moisture to it ~ otherwise your would have worked in vain. Therefore take care that the mercury does not rise, for every live Mercury contains much water, as you will notice in the receptacle. That must be removed from it if it is to die with Gold and Silver and turn into a fixed powder. But if it were to retain its moisture, it would never die completely. Therefore, draw its moisture off as long as you see moisture appear in the alembic. Then let it stand for 10 days and watch that it does not sublimate. After this, take it out and preserve it in a glass or can, in a warm place, well closed to prevent any moisture from getting into it.

My child must know that all Mercury intended to be used for amalgamating must be prepared in this way, as otherwise it will not die or will congeal. This has led many a man astray, so that he did not achieve his purpose on account of the excess of water contained in Mercury. And thus they remain mistaken.

You should further know that Sol, Luna, and Mercury must be prepared in this way to achieve a better conjunction. Weigh your powder of Sol and Luna, add to it their weight in prepared Mercury, and no more, for if you take more, your work will have to stand all the longer in the fire. But if there is no more of one ingredient than of another, the spirit will die next to the Body and be congealed and brought to its perfect color, be it for the White or the Red. After that, pour a large amount of Mercury over it, to increate and liquify the Stone.

On the fixed White Stone you must pour about 10 or 12 parts of Spirit, and one Red about 20 or 24, even up to 30 parts. For if you take 12 parts of Spirit to one part of the White, one part of the Red requires at least 30 parts before it becomes fusible, the reason begin that the White Stone is raw, moist, cold, and white. It therefore does not need half as much Paradise Water, or Spirit, to increase it as the Red which is hot and dry in its nature, and before it begins to melt, it requires about 30 parts of Spirit to one part of Stone. Someone might ask: If we have to pour so much paradise Water on the white and the red powder before they become liquid and subtle, they must probably stand a long time in the fire before the Spirit of both can ripen and die and become fixed with the Stone.

This is so because in their innermost composition both Spirit and Body were raw, and they must therefore stand longer before they can penetrate and embrace each other in their depths.

The first amalgamation must be made with such a small fire that little or nothing can rise in the vessel in which it is contained, It must therefore stand for a long time before it dies and turns into powder. And when the Stone to the White and the Red is made, it is fixed and not liquid, and is yet a medicine at bottom, although it has no ingress yet.

Hermes says: When Mercury is dissolved, it dissolves only a little of the other metals and spirits, and when it is coagulated, it continues to coagulate.

And Hermes says further: Even if much Paradise Water is poured over it, yes, even 30 parts to one part of already coagulated Mercury, it coagulates this Paradise Water somewhat.

Another reason is the following: Part of the powder is already a medicine, though it cannot be melted and it therefore turns some of the Paradise Water into its own nature. Also, if the Paradise water is poured on the powder and put in the furnace, it may be heated much more than at the beginning of the Work ~ because at the beginning it must not sublimate. Now you can heat it so that it rises and again falls back on the powder in droplets. As soon as it begins to die and turn into powder, increase you fire to make it sublimate, and turn the glass frequently upside down, so that the matter above falls to the bottom, Continue doing this till everything stays together below. After that, raise the fire somewhat till it gets its color, be it to the White or to the Red.

These are the reasons why one has to pour so much Paradise Water on one part of the powder. It must not stand as long as in the beginning of the work, this is so that you should rightly understand the Work, know what is good and what is bad, and not go wrong. Be cautious, therefore, and know what to do, enclose it in your heart and memory and reflect upon it before beginning anything that might be harmful to your work.

Now we will do the Work. Take the powder Sol and Luna, weigh it, add to it as much Philosophical Mercury as above, put it onto an iron mortar, heat it, but not so much that the Mercury rises, add to it in English weight of *, well pulverized. Then pound it into an amalgamate with the *, which absorbs the red powder and the Mercury. Pound it thus ceaselessly for a whole day, and the next day pound it again ceaselessly for 12 hours, but block your mouth, nose and ears to that you do not get hurt by it. After these 12 hours, put your matter in a glass with its mouth tightly closed, set it in the secret furnace and give it fire in due form, as has been taught in the Great Work. By regulating the fire, you will accomplish all the works connected with the amalgamate.

It is all a regimen of the fire, but it is done in various ways. Yet they all achieve results ~ but each is seeking to shorten the time. There have been some others who took the Stone which God has given us for nothing. They sublimated and purified it of all its faeces three or four times, the coagulated it again into a white powder and preserved it in a little box till they needed it. The Stone was ready. Now they took the prepared Mercury, sublimated it with vitriol, mixed one lb of Mercury and 3 lb of vitriol and elevated it. After this, they again ground the Mercury among the faces and sublimated it again.

28

The third time, they took 2 lb of fresh vitriol ~ throwing away the other faeces ~ sublimed it again, and put it in a tightly closed box. Then they took 15 oz Luna and 5 oz Sol, melted them together, filed it small and pounded it in a mortar. After this, the powder was washed clean, dried again and also preserved in a box. Now they took 8 Lots of the Stone which God has given us for nothing, 4 Lots of the gold and silver powder, and as much sublimated Mercury as their combined weight, to make it 24 Lots all together. They mixed all this and pounded it on a stone till it became intangible, dried it on hot ashes, put it into a round glass thus formed (see the drawing), and filled it to the brim. They hung it in tripodem in the innermost room, closed it and let it hang for 84 days, and they gave it only so much fire that they could easily put their hand in it without getting burnt. They did this by means of a lamp. When the 84 days were over, they took the glass from the stove, broke it and removed the mater. They then heated a copper plate, put the matter on it and set it in a blacksmith's furnace. They watched to see if the matter was smoking and if it had lost any weight, or they put half a Lot into a crucible, let it become red-hot for a quarter of an hour, then weighed it again to see if they had lost some. If they noticed a loss, they put the matter once more into a glass, and in tripodem, gave it a somewhat stronger fire than before ~ so that one could hardly put one's hand in it ~ and let it stand for another 30 or 40 days. Then they removed the glass and looked if the matter was fixed. And without it, it will be fixed and red like blood, and will not flow.

Now they took the matter and mixed it with 2 parts of the philosophical Paradise Water in a hot mortar, and ground it for 12 hours without stopping. Then they put it in such a glass as is illustrated here, closed with strong lute, put it on the furnace and let it rise and fall till everything was turned into powder. They continued doing this till everything was fixed together and stayed at the bottom. This done, they left it there at the same regimen of the fire till the white color appeared. When it was white, they had the White Elixir; but if they whished to have the Red Elixir, they let it stand and increased the fire, as with the regimen of the fire to the White the redness does not emerge, as mentioned before. That is why we must understand and remember everything very well if we wish to be perfect and act perfectly in the Art and produce something useful. Therefore do not begrudge reading this over frequently in order to understand. When then the redness appears, you have accomplished the Red Elixir for the transmutation of all imperfect metals into genuine gold, better than the natural one. It can stand all tests and examinations.

In addition, you should know that everything I shall report and teach about this Work is to be understood as concerning the Great Work (the Magnum Opus) of which the philosophers have written in covert words. First, there is the reduction of the Body to its first nature: They amalgamated the perfect Body, that is Luna (because it is fixed) and this is the solution of the old masters. Their dissolution is not achieved by pouring rain water on the Body but a very dry Water, which is Mercury. This is the foundation of the Art of which Rhasis says: Unless you dissolve the Body, you work in vain.

Of this dissolution Geber says in his *Liber Veritatis* in the *Turba*: The surest way lies in the art of reduction, that is, the dissolution of the Bodies into a clear beautiful water out of which they were first generated. In this water the Spirit, Soul and Body are contained.

Geber says further: When they turned the Bodies into mercury in such a way that they could pass through a cloth, they said, Now we have an Element of Fire.

Further, he says that the earth is made out of the coarseness of the water, and that they said: We have also the other Elements, Fire and Earth.

The third work is purification, of which Morienus says: The earth is rotten because of the water, and it has to be purified. Then, with God's help, the whole magistrery has been accomplished.

The *Turba Philosophorum* says: Moisten the dry with the wet, because the dry is the earth and the wet is the water; see now, we have purified the water and the earth.

The fourth work is the evaporation of the water. When the Water of Paradise rises to heaven and falls down again to the earth in droplets, they call it sublimation. By rising and falling it turns into powder, and they call this rising Air. Thus you have Water, Air and Earth, and that is as the philosophers say: When it has become white, pour Paradise Water over it and let it sublimate until it turns into a spirit called Bird of Hermes. Morienus says of it: Do not despise the ashes, for you will find at the bottom a shining ash, and in it you will find a precious adamant.

After this they say: Add to it the Ferment Aleph.

To turn it into a white powder, it must be imbibed with Paradise Water in which fine gold should be amalgamated. They call this imbibing, fermenting. Further, the philosophers say: Moisten the body with the soul.

Therefore we add the soul to the Stone, for just as a man's body is not without a soul, our Stone is not without a soul and life. The soul purifies the imperfect body because it adds the ferment to nature. That is why they add a ferment when the fold is mingled with the Paradise Water. It is as Morienus says: Unless you purify and whiten the powders perfectly, then infuse the soul into them and unite it with the powders, you have not done anything toward your magistery.

That is why the philosopher Bautin says: Join the soul to the body and the spirit.

Then the spirit will be added and they will rejoice together, for they have been transformed from their nature ∼ a coarse thing ∼ and have now become subtle. It is this of which the philosophers say in the *Codex Veritatis*: The spirits are not combined with the body until they are completely rid of their impurity.

In this conjunction there are wonderful things, because all the colors of the world, as many as you can think of, are contained in it, and finally all merge into one color, which is the red. Then the body is colored by the ferment, which is the soul, and the spirit with the soul are joined to the body and is again converted with it into the colors of the ferment, so that the fire can no loner separate it, no matter how strong it may be.

From what I have told you, you can understand that the philosophers spoke the truth: Our Stone is composed of body soul, and spirit.

They considered the perfect body a dead body, because Luna is sick and not fixed. They say that the spirit is a running, glistening water, and they call the sol the ferment. They speak of the truth, for it gives life to the body, which it did not have before, and gives it a better form. And thus everything they have written in covert words is true.

In addition, some philosophers say: Unless you make the corporeal incorporeal, and the incorporeal corporeal, you have done nothing in our Art.

When it is amalgamated, we first make water of the body, then the body is disembodied. By constant decoction it becomes drunk and dies with the spirit ~ then the spirit turns into a body.

The old masters say: Follow Nature, and you will find what you are looking for.

It is true, for in our Work we first make the moist dry, or the coarse subtle, then the subtle coarse, a spirit out of the body, and a body out of the spirit. Of the uppermost we make the lowest, and of the lowest the uppermost. Thus they transform one nature into another, just as it is supposed to be.

That the old masters described this in such obscure words, however, is because of the unwise who are not Sons of the Art, so that they should not understand it, as it is meant to be a secret.

It is also the reason why they wrote so many chapters, to make the unintelligent believe that our Art is so difficult. In every chapter they wrote about foreign things, including many foreign names, such as reductio, solutio, ablutio, sublimatio, destillatio, coagulatio, calcinations, fixation, and various other names and manipulations, as I said before.

Observe Now How the Ancients Found Such Terms in the Work

If you wish to make a Work as the old masters, our forefathers, did, take Mercury that comes out of the earth where they dig for old or silver, and not artificially manufactured quicksilver. Press it through leather, and if something is left in the leather, see what body it is. Melt it in a crucible with borax and you will see with what kind of metal it is mixed. If it is an imperfect metal, the Mercury is of no use for our Work, but if you find Gold or Silver, it is good. If you do not find any body at all, it is also good.

Take as much of this Mercury as you like. Put it in a glass vessel, an alembic on top, and draw the superfluous moisture from it, as it would be harmful in your Work. After this, take the perfect body, well refined of led in the cupel, and amalgamate it with a large amount of Mercury. The old masters always took 3 parts of silver and 1 part of gold. They called it the Ferment. Some of the old ones amalgamated gold and silver together, as has been taught before.

Others, however, amalgamated only gold with the Paradise Water and finally poured it on the powder; to the ferment, as will be described later. When they amalgamated silver, they put it in a glass (as illustrated) in tripodem, in all whiteness, as was taught in the previous chapter, and with the same regimen of the fire. In this way they also amalgated gold and put it in a glass in tripodem, like silver. The Paradise Water came from Mercury whose moisture had been drawn off. Hey put the latter likewise in a glass and set it in tripodem to the other two glasses till the Work had incerated. They did this so that it would more easily incerate and stick to the Work, because it becomes half-fixed, having been decocted for so long. But it has not yet turned into powder, and even if it were to stand in the furnace for 10 years, it would not die.

That is why Mercurius says: If as much of myself as a fish-eye were alive, I would not be dead.

The reason is that no body has been mixed with it; neither father nor mother nor someone of its species has been added to it in the amalgamation. This you should understand as follows: If a metal or a metallic Spirit is intermixed with Mercury or some of our White or Red Stone ~ which are of its species ~ it will die at once, but it will never die alone by itself.

Dear children, Read this lesson over often, so that you may learn to know the nature of all things ~ and let this be said enough.

Now we will return to our Work, which we had left. All three glasses are standing in tripode, in the innermost chamber ~ which is to be carefully sealed to prevent any air from escaping ~ and are governed by a fire so small that you can put your hand in it for half an hour without burning. Now the old masters wondered how they could give a special sign for each sign they saw in the Work, so that the fools who were no Sons of the Art would not understand it. Therefore they gave so many names and wrote about so many different manipulations to make it appear all too difficult, such as solutio, inceratio, and various other labors. And all this only because of the ignorant who are not children of the Art and are not to possess the heritage of the wise.

This whole operation takes place in a closed glass, with the Work standing in the furnace. The fools learn that each operation is a special work, to be prepared in special glasses and with special instruments, with strange oils and a difficult regimen of the fire. They consider it difficult and cannot understand that everything can be accomplished in one closed vessel, in one furnace, and with one regimen of the fire.

First, the old masters saw that the matter or the Stone developed a black skin or blackness. They wondered how they should call it and decided to call it a blackening of the sea or the lake, as the water was all black above. And as Sol and Luna were in it, they called it the Solar and Lunar Eclipse — and the fools did not understand it.

Secondly, they saw that the water — which is Mercury — was rising above in the glass out of the matter and the body of Sol and Luna. Then they said: The wind carried it in its belly — because it rises out of the warmth of the matter.

Therefore, a philosopher says: You must add it to the Air, in whose belly it is to be carried through the action of the sun, which is its father. After that, give it to drink Aleph when it falls down again to the bottom or on the matter, for it is to be imbibed with the moisture of the earth which is its nurse.

Regarding this, Hermes, a father of the philosophers, says as follows: What is above is like what is below, and what is below, is like what is above.

Dandin says: Whoever wishes to perform miracles with a thing of which our Stone is the father and the earth is the sister, and Luna the mother, and the wind carries it in its belly, and its nurse is the earth...

Further says the same philosopher: It rises from the earth to heaven, and from heaven back to the earth, and it shall get power from what is above and what is below.

He speaks the truth, for when it begins to hang above in drops and those fall back on the earth, it dies and turns into a powder. When it is such, you must pour Paradise Water over it and then present Luna, which is now its nourishment, and heat it till your thing is completed. Now it is more precious than anything in the world. But the ignorant cannot understand it. When the old masters saw that it continued rising and falling in the glass, they reflected and found no other name for this than Sublimate, because it is a true sublimation.

Therefore Geber says in the Turba: When the Stone or the Work is conjoined, it is ready for sublimation...

The fools did not understand that the sublimation takes place in a closed glass, and they erred.

Further, they noticed that the droplets fell down and remained as water, and they called this Distillation. That is why Morienus says in the Buch der Scharen: After the sublimation follows the distillation.

Finally, the matter is transformed into earth, and the earth stays on the water. It happens as follows: When Mercury rose, it moved out of the matter or the earth, and when it fell down, it did no mingle again with the body and slowly turned into earth. At last they noticed that the earth again began to sink below the water to the bottom of the vessel, and in so doing it turned black. They thought they would call it the Corruption and the Fetid monster. Of this

Morienus says in his books: Our Stone is found in a rotten corrupted monster, that is where our Stone is gathered.

From this some concluded that the Stone should be sought in stables, troughs, dirt, manure. They were mistaken, because they are not or children.

After this, they saw this evil-smelling earth die by means of constant coction and a good regimen of the fire. The water lost its stench and changed colors. The philosophers call this the Ablution. That is why Morienus says: Wash the original matter and purify the evil-smelling substance with the water. That is why they calcined it with salt, pounded it on a stone, washed it with pure water, and did this till the water ran off quite pure. And they were as far ahead with their Work as when they began, and lost money, effort, and labor.

Hermes and Geber say: Know that our Art is nothing but a drawing of the water out of the earth and a pouring of the water back on it, till they are both washed and mixed together.

The ignorant do not know that this must be done in a closed vessel, in our furnace, because they are not our children.

After this, they saw this evil-smelling earth die by means of constant coction and a good regimen of the fire. The water lost its stench and changed colours. The philosophers call this the Ablution. That is why Morienus says: Wash the original matter and purify the evil-smelling substance with the water. Then a conjunction may occur between body, soul, and spirit ~ and the ignorant thought that the body had to be washed with common water. That is why they calcined it with salt, pounded it on a stone, washed it with pure water, and did all this till the water ran off quite pure. And they were as far ahead with their Work as when they began, and lost money, effort, and labor.

Hermes and Geber say: Know that our Art s nothing but a drawing of the water our of the earth and mixed together.

The ignorant do not understand this and stick to their fantasies. They do not know that this must be done in a closed glass, in our furnace, because they are not our children.

Then, after a long decoction and regimen of the fire, the philosophers saw that the earth grew and became coarser, thereafter smaller, due to the tempered heat. Now they all said, It is a perfect inceration.

That was its proper name, and therefore Dandin the Philosopher says: One should extract its strength and imbibe it again.

Hermes says: The earth is to be imbibed with the water.

Morienus: Give to drink to the thirsty till it has enough juice, and it will no more be thirsty in all eternity.

The ignorant do not understand that it all takes pace in a closed glass by a long decoction and tempered heat.

Then they noticed that all the water was dry and had turned into earth. Geber says: When our earth is made, our magistery is accomplished for the most part.

They saw the matter turn into a thick, hard substance, and when it stood firm and did no longer rise, they said: This is a perfect coagulation, made of its own matter.

Hermes says: Dissolve our Stone and coagulate it very carefully, turn it into earth, and thereafter make it white, then alive, and finally red ~ and you have the magistery.

Dandin says: Know that our Stone is nothing but a perfect dissolving and again coagulating without a change of its substance, without taking anything away from it or adding anything to it. Till you have done everything, shun all books and do not seek anything else.

Morienus says: Our work is nothing but a woman's work and children's play.

Stupid men cannot understand it and do not know how the secret words are to be understood, but if they were our children, they would understand and know everything clearly.

Further, they saw that by a long decoction and tempered hat the earth became increasingly white, and finally they saw it became completely brilliant, and its whiteness surpassed all the whiteness in the world. They called this whitening Calcination, and it is truly the right calcinations of the forefathers and the right name.

That is why Hermes and Morienus say: Do not despise the ash that lies at the bottom, for in it is a precious adamant and a maid who will be surrounded by fruit and bring forth a Son of Life.

When now the ferment is mixed with the white earth, the imperfect body or earth receives the ferment, and then is accomplished what one intended to do. This is what the old philosophers mean when they say: Feed the child with its own milk till it is grown up.

It means that the white earth should be incerated with the ferment and the Paradise Water. As this matter was white and fixed, they removed it from the furnace together with the other glass containing the gold amalgamate, pounded them together in a stone mortar with a steel pestle to mix them well, and in this way they fermented. Concerning this, Morienus says: Conjoin and add its soul to it, so that it may not part from the body in all eternity.

Geber says: Arrange a marriage and put the bride to bed with her bridegroom, and imbibe both with the dew of heaven, and the bride will conceive a son who will be kin over all his line, and all his enemies will make peace with him, and he will be crowned with a red diadem.

After this, they took the matter and put it back into the glass, took the Paradise Water and imbibed the matter with 10 parts of Paradise Water to 1 part of matter, and that is as Geber says: Moisten the bed with heavenly dew, and the bride will conceive a son.

Thereafter they sealed the glass, put it back into the furnace and increased the fire somewhat till the Paradise Water sublimated and fell back in the earth in drops. That was the Son who makes everything brilliant and who is to be fed with his own milk till he is grown up.

My child, You should know and well understand that if you wish to make the red Ston, you must bring the white earth to redness by its ferment and by increasing the fire till the earth turns yellow. When it is perfectly yellow, like a crocus, the Element Air comes out. With the regimen of the fire which drives out and moves the Air, the fire cannot brig out the red tincture, unless it be greatly increased till the matter turns red. When it is red, imbibe it wit Paradise Water till it has absorbed it all and has turned into a powder. Now regulate the fire till the powder becomes white once more, like snow; then increase the fire till it becomes yellow again, and every more till the matter becomes red ~ and now your Work is ready and accomplished.

In this Work you have all four Elements, each separately. First you have seen Water and earth. They appeared first, and the Air was removed from them, which you also saw later in the yellowness. Now you see the Fire in its redness, because it is now on the outside.

The old masters spoke the truth, saying that our Stone is made of four Elements. Neverthelesss, it was no more than one, and made of one thing, and they spoke the truth. But if you only want the White Stone, give it Paradise Water, just as you did with the ferment, let it ascend and descend till it stays at the bottom, keep up the regimen of the fire till the powder again becomes perfectly white, and you have the perfect white Stone for the transmutation of all imperfect bodies into true silver. Consequently, my child should know that all these methods of operation are good, and their projection so high as to amaze you, and you will discover it yourself.

If you throw your good medicine on a metal or on mercury, as long as the medicine retains its power, the metal is frangible like glass that can be pulverized. If you now throw some of this powder on another metal, it is still a medicine, and in this way it should always be thrown on other metals, as much as the projection allows, be it on gold or on silver, according to how the medicine is prepared.

Thereafter they sealed the glass, put it back into the furnace and increased the fire somewhat till the Paradise Water sublimated and fell back on the earth in drops. That was the Son who makes everything brilliant and who is to be fed with his own milk till he is grown up.

My child, You should know and well understand that if you wish to make the red Stone, you must bring the white earth to redness by its ferment and by increasing the fire till the earth turns yellow. When it is perfectly yellow, like a crocus, the element Air comes out. With the regimen of the fire which drives out and moves the Air, the fire cannot bring out the red tincture, unless it be greatly increased till the matter turns red. When then it is red, imbibe it with Paradise Water till it has absorbed it all and has turned into a powder. Now regulate the fire till the powder becomes white once more, like snow; then increase the fire till it becomes yellow again, and ever more till the matter becomes red ~ and now your Work is ready and accomplished.

In this Work you have seen all four Elements, each separately. First you have seen Water and earth. They appeared first, and the Air was removed from them, which you also saw later in the yellowness. Now you see the Fire in its redness, because it is now on the outside.

The old masters spoke the truth, saying that our Stone is made of four Elements. Nevertheless, it was no more than one, and made of one thing, and they spoke the truth. But if you only want the white Stone, give it Paradise Water, just as you did with the ferment, let it ascend and descend till it stays at the bottom, keep up the regimen of the fire till the powder again becomes perfectly white, and you have the perfect white Stone for the transmutation of all imperfect bodies into true silver. Consequently, my child should know that all these methods of operation are good, and their projection so high as to amaze you, and you will discover it yourself.

If you throw your medicine on a metal or on mercury, as long as the medicine retains its power, the metal is frangible like glass that can be pulverized. If you now throw some of this powder on another metal, it is still a medicine, and in this way it should always be thrown on other metals, as much as the projection allows, be it on gold or on silver, according to how the medicine is prepared.

Multiplication of the Stone

Now I will teach you how you should multiply the Stone. You must not make the Stone more than once in your life, after which you may make of it as much as you wish, even in the hundred pounds and more.

Take 10 or 12 lb Mercury, sublimate it through Roman Vitriol, 3 parts of vitriol to 1 part of Mercury. When the Mercury is ready, preserve it till you need it. Then take 1 oz of fine gold, cement it in the regal, and make it in the crucible. Throw into it 1 oz of your medicine, let it melt a little, about the time it takes to say two Pater Nosters. Then it is a mass, which take out, pound into a subtle powder, and grind on a stone with rectified vinegar. This is done so that the powder may dry somewhat on a small fire, because wine flies away as soon as it feels the heat. Now take the powder, add to it its weight in mercury, mix them well together, quite dry, on stone, then grind it with rectified vinegar. Dry it in the sun or in a room to remove all moisture, put it in a glass as illustrated, pour on it 12 parts of mercury, close the glass tightly, shake it by hand to mix the mercury and the powder, set it in tripodem, give it fire as has been taught, and immediately as hot as it was when you poured on the Paradise Water, and let it stand for 40 days.

Then it will all be a medicine, and it is as good and better than it was before. If you wish to make more medicine, take a large glass, weigh 10 oz of your Medicine and add 100 oz of mercury, prepared as above, that is, of which the moisture has been removed. Mix well, set it in tripodem for 40 days with the above regimen of the fire, and it will all turn into medicine as good as the first. Thus you can multiply your medicine ad infinitum in a short time, and it is always as good as the first.

Further my child should know that there were some who took 9 parts of prepared Paradise Water and 1 part of the Stone. They put it into 9 phials well sealed and set it in tripodem in the innermost chamber till the Stone was ready and the Paradise Water had to be poured on it. After this, they took one phial out and poured it into the Paradise Water, mixed well, stoppered it well with lute and set it again in its place. They let the other 8 parts stand where they were till part of the Stone had become fixed. Thus they did with all 9 glasses till all imbibed their portion of Paradise Water and had thereby become fixed. This seems to me to be the best method as it shortens the Work and is easy to do because it is not as overloaded as if everything were put together in one glass. True, it requires somewhat more work but it better to pour on these 9 parts than on one part of the Stone, and that is what the old masters did and what they taught their children. Hear and understand these words, for they spoke thus: Take 9 parts of May Dew, each sealed in a phial and keep in the tripod in even heat till the lowest part becomes white and dry, then imbibe the lowest with p. 1 part 6 parts of May Dew, and then with the other part, till it flows like oil.

You must know that the old alchemists made the Stone in many different ways, and at the end it was always good. Know that the old masters worked as I have told you. But their descendants discovered many other forms of the works by which they could shorten the Art, such as using aquafort, as is being taught in the Mineral Work at many different places. Likewise in the Animal Work and even much more so in the Vegetable Work, which are all full of wonders, and strange waters which seem to be miraculous, as is being taught at many places in the Vegetable Work. They also discovered how to separate the Elements in various ways, as is also taught in the Work at many places, and it has to be done with great subtility and care. They also sought to shorten the time and to try doing it according to Nature. The Work involves great worry, much labor and much expense and uncertainty. Therefore I advise you, my dear children, avoid all works requiring the separation of the Elements or many ways of making AF, as I have taught in the preface and will teach later.

We have taught how our forefathers dealt with the amalgamate, and as they all reached a sure conclusion, the product was of such a goodness, it could not be improved upon.

Now I Will Teach You How To Make The Stone From Putrefied Water As Well As How To Make The Olea of Metals.
This Can Be Done With Little Effort And Without Separation Of The Elements.
You Will Also Learn The Method Of Bringing Them To Such A Perfection As Is Certain And Good.

The reason why the Elements are separated is that the Imperfectum be made perfect; also that the impurities be separated, and that the corpus and spirit be this rid of all impurity, and be afterwards conjoined. Know then, that anything that reaches the fire, no matter how impure it is, is made clean and pure by the fire, as we have taught before. The first sign is a perfect blackness, and we see it with out eyes. All matter becomes as black as pitch. Why? The fire drives Corruption, or what is rotten, upwards and it leaves the matter because of the strength of the heat. This is not done, however, with a strong but with a gentle fire. Then the Corruption of Faces which in the Arca are driven above until everything is black.

That is why Morienus says: Take care that you regulate your fire in such a way that you do not obtain whiteness before blackness, the albedo before the nigredo, or all your work is spoiled by the whiteness if it occurs before the blackness.

So it must be a sure method that will drive the Corruption out by fire, and thus must be the purification and Perfection. Be careful in our work for after long and steady boiling the heat consumes the Corruption, faeces and blackness, and changes it into another color, and ever another until it is perfectly white like snow. And it is done gently, so that the elements are not forced, but are gently rectified of their impurities. Take care, however, in every respect, as Morienus has warned, tat you do not get the redness before the whiteness; for our Stone must not be burnt in this work. Know that this is the best way; for it is often necessary to give strong heat where the separation of the elements must be accomplished, before the elementum ignis is brought over, and everything must glow.

After this, if you wish to calcine the faeces the matter has to be burnt in the reverberating furnace. Often the matte turns white; then it has to be changed into glass, and thus one thing is spoilt with the other. But, in the Great Work, there is no uncertainty. The faeces know how to consume themselves of themselves, as Geber says: The dragon must devour its own blackness, and it has to be fed with its own venom. Dantin says: The black crow must hatch its own eggs with its young, till they all turn white For that is the art and nature of all things under the sky, that they desire to rectify themselves out of an inherent impulse and to rid themselves of their faeces which are superfluous to them, and to be without defect. For they were perfect and without defects from the beginning. The four Elementa, and everything made from them, mobile and immobile, nothing excepted, are all perfect in the beginning and in the end, and all things desire to be rid of the faeces.

Someone might ask: But what are the faeces? It is a humor or moisture which God has ordered, and everything under the course of heaven must be nourished by it. It keeps all things in its nature and is in all things a perfect, elementary, natural warmth or fire, and if the perfect fire does not meet with unfortunate accidents, it will keep the thing in its nature. But as soon as a bad accident happens to the fire, which is also hot and imperfect, and one thing mingles with another, they all become hot and harm and destroy the thing, be it in metals, animas, trees or herbs, and in all things under the sky.

There two kinds of water in all things created out of the Elements, a natural one and an elementary one, and that is perfect, good and eternal. Then there is still another water. It is called the Water of the Clouds. That is imperfect, and is mixed with the elementary water. It is meant to give nourishment and moisture to things and to keep them in their nature as long as no other extraneous water is added to them. But if more is added, it will drown the thing, so that it dies and corrupts, just as when water is poured into fire.

Similarly, you must understand this in regard to air and earth. If there were no faeces in the elements, all things would be perfect, spiritual and subtle, as God meant them to be. Nor would there be decaying and death, as is explained about faeces and diseases of the elements in the Vegetablili. Find it in Chapter 16.

Now you might ask, however; if a thing is destroyed in such a way, where then is the perfection which it contains? Read about that in the Vegetabili, Chapter 29. You will also find explained there how one thing attracts its like. Know also that, if a thing has died, be it sensitive or insensitive, the spirit of its corpus separates from it and joins its like, from which it has originated, as you will understand by the Vegetabili. Look at the flame of fire or coal; the flames heat, the smoke moves upward. In this smoke is hidden the spirit of air. It joins its like. The same applies to the other elements.

But now someone may ask: Where then do the faeces elementorum stay, when each thing has gone to its own?

Concerning this, consider this example: If you put a glass vessel containing water into the sun the sun draws the water to itself, and stinking black dregs will stay behind. Let it stand in the glass protected from rain and wind, for a long time, and the slimy black matter will in time become white as snow and is smell will disappear. Such is the effect of the nature of the sun. Another example: Take a glass basin full of green herbs; put it in the sun or exposed to the air. The herbs will begin to decay and smell bad, and, each element draws towards its like as mentioned before. The black stinking earth stays in the basin, but after a long time the air and the warmth of the sun will calcine it as white as snow, And this is the work of nature.

Another example: Take the corpse of an evildoer, who lies on the rack or hangs on the gallows. The air and the sun consume its stench and decay, so that nothing remains but white ashes. In time the hard legs, which were full of fat and marrow, are thus consumed, so that they turn into white, fine salt which is intangible between the fingers. That is brought about by nature, as we may see every day with our own eyes. Where then remains the stinking matter? It passes away and turns into nothing, and the element earth is thus cleansed and white as snow, so that it becomes impalpable. Thus it is evident in our Art one must not separate any elements, nor does one require any washing or purification.

That is has to be tested to ascertain that it is good and penetrating I have related to you so that you should understand that the separationes elementorum are not necessary in our work. Neither is rectification, because the faeces consume themselves, as indicated: but in the separations elementorum, a little is always lost in the fire, for they stand in the fire. And just as it easily loses something, so it is to the detriment of the work, which you need not be afraid of in this instance, because in the Great Work no element is separated.

In addition, you should also know that one can make oil from all metals also without separation of the elements, and without much washing and dissolving. Yet, it must be done with Aqua Fortis, and you must give it a ferment, if you wish to make them from a perfect metal. But I advise you not to make oil from any imperfect metal, except from lead and tin, one for the Red, the other for the White. There exist many different matters, from which to make oil. They have been discovered due to the rapidity in which they can be made, while some did not have the patience to endure the long amount of time required to accomplish the great Work and because they seek small gain. Yet in such things there is great danger, more than in the Great work, also greater labor and handicraft. You must distill AF, and you must also sublimate and be well acquainted with many unusual types of work. It also requires a great deal of money, effort, and cost.

The Other Works of the Ancient Philosophers

Olea Ex Aquis Fortibus et Metallis

(An Oil from Aquafort and Luna)

There were some who made an Aqua Fort from Vitriol and Sol. In it they dissolved fine Luna one part, of the cupel. After that, they ground it and washed the calx off with common water; then they dried it in the sun or with fire. Afterward, they put this calx into two glasses, poured rectified vinegar upon it, each time 1 lb of vinegar upon 1 ounce of calx lunae. They put one of the glasses in the balneum and the other in front of it. Then they distilled the vinegar from one Luna onto the other, alternating the glasses; one into the balneum, the other one, which had been standing before it, out. Then they distilled once more, and did this until the Luna was fully dissolved.

When the Luna is totally dissolved, the Aqua Vitae has to be drawn off in the balneum with gentle heat, such that one can suffer one's hand to be in this heat. When a skin forms on the Luna, the process must be stopped, allow it to cool down and put into a cold cellar to crystallize. Take out the crystals formed and put them in a small retort, lute it well and set it in warm ashes in tripodem, or let it stand until the clear little stones have been transformed into oil with it ad album.

Another Kind of Oil Made from Aquafort and Luna

There have been also others who took 1 oz of Luna amalgamated with prepared Mercury, in such a way that the amalgamation could be pressed through a linen cloth. After that, they set it for 6 weeks in moderate heat; and they dissolved it in an AF made of Vitriol and Salt; drew off again gently in the balneum. Then they removed it, stoppered it well, set it in cinerum or tripodem and gave it heat as if one wished to keep Lead in flux. They kept it thus until the oil was fixed, and tested it in the following way: They took a sheet of Copper and heated it to glowing, then poured one drop of this oil upon it. If the oil goes through without smoke, like oil through leather, and if it tinges to Silver, it is fixed, good and a perfect elixir. But if it does not do that, put it back in tripodem until it is fixed and transmutes Mercury, Tin and Copper into true Silver, which passes all tests.

An Oil Made from Aquafort and Jupiter

Take 1 lb if Roman Vitriol, 5 lb of auripigment sublimated to the White, 1 lb of Mercury sublimated to the White, calx of tin, 1 lb of (+) ad pondus omnium. Mix them well together with vinegar, like a paint, then dry the matter in the sun. Now divide the matter into 3 parts, of one part of which prepare an AF. Pour it thereafter on the second part and distill it again with a strong fire. Finally you must pulverize all three death's heads, put the substance in a glass, pour the AF on it, lute an alembic and a receptacle in front and let it stand thus in ash for 8 days before you give fire, to allow the water to incorporate well with the earth. Now light the fire and keep it going slowly for 24 hours. Thereafter increase it from degree to degree, as you well know, so that it slowly becomes red-hot after 24 hours. Let it stand thus for another 24 hours, then give it as strong a fire as it can stand, for 3 days and nights. Even if the glass were to break, it would not matter. Then let it go down, remove the water and preserve it well sealed, because it is a precious water, better than gold.

Take the Death's Head, grind it to a powder and pound it quite finely on a stone with distilled vinegar. Put it in a stone jar, pour on it a good amount of distilled vinegar and set it in the Balneum for 8 days, stirring it well with a wooden spoon every day. Then stopper it again. Finally, let it settle, pour what is above off into another vessel, put an alembic on it and distill the vinegar to complete dryness. A white earth will be left behind. Dissolve it again in vinegar, put it again in a boiling Balneum and let it dissolve and evaporate once more. Continue doing this till there are no more faces, and your salt will be more beautiful than snow. Keep it till you need it.

Now take 1 lb of copper and 1 oz of silver, some prepared gem salt, which I have taught to prepare at other places. Take also mercury and auripigment, of each 1 oz, and as much salt as you have of the salt which I asked you to prepare from the water. Mix everything and pound it quite impalpably on a stone with vinegar. Then put it in a glass dish, dry it in a room or in the sun, and when it is quite dry, pound it again on a stone. Then put it in a retort, lute an alembic on it that has a hole on top, set it in a Balneum, put a receptacle in front, and give it as much fire that you could hold your hand in the Balneum. Pour your aqua fortis on the matter through a funnel. Slowly distill the water off, and when nothing comes over any more, let it cool, pour some water on it, draw it off again, and do this till nothing of the water goes over any longer. Then remove the alembic, put it in ash or in the tripod, the glass closed with a good lute, let it stand for 6 weeks, and give it so much fire that you could hardly hold your hand in the furnace for the duration of one Pater Noster. At the end of 6 weeks, test it on a copper foil. If it passes through without smoke and tinges it into silver, it is a perfect Elixir. But if it des not do so, put it back in the tripod as before until it passes the test. Then you have a perfect oil for transmuting the imperfect metals into silver. Its projection is one part to 1000 parts, because it is a very powerful oil. I have seen it do wonders, and consider this oil a minor medicine.

A Recipe (For a Projective Powder)

Found in a casket walled in a wall, sold for much money. It is genuine and quite expert, as those will easily recognize who are experiences in alchemy and learned in the process. Therefore, take care not to reveal this secret to the greedy and ostentatious or to those who are not children of the Philosophy. Begin as follows:

Take, in the name of our Lord Jesus Christ, as much gold as you like, make an amalgam with one part of mercury, evaporate the mercury with a small fire, then reverbarate it for 20 days and nights, grind it very small, pour good distilled rectified vinegar, 4 fingers breadth, over the material. Stopper the cucurbit carefully and set it on hot ashes for 2 days and nights. Thereafter the vinegar will take on a red color from the gold, Reverbarate it again for 9 days as before, each time reverberating less, and each tine pouring carefully the colored vinegar together. Do this till all your gold is resolved into a grey powder, which is no good for anything. I did this also, but I took aquafortis, so as to dissolve it the more easily.

Distill the solution, and you will find your gold salt at the bottom. Reverbarate it for 12 hours (as the recipe demands), which I did, but I regretted it, because the spirit left by more than half. If I had known this, I could have obtained and caught the spirit.

Aftr this, dissolve the gold in rectified aqua vitae, let it stand, as has been said about the vinegar. What is not dissolved, reverbarate for 3 days and 3 nights, and when all your gold is dissolved in the aqua vitae, pour the solutions together, distill the aqua vitae off, and you will find a beautiful salt at the bottom, which dissolves immediately just as the salt *. Of this salt take 1 part to 4 parts, put some live coal on it and under it, and in half an hour you will find mercury calcined to a powder. But I did not succeed in this. What hindered me was (I believe) the salt, because the spiritus, as I said, had escaped in the reverbaration during the 12 preceding hours.

This Work Cost 800 Guilders

O child of the Doctrine! First seek the kingdom of God, obedience to the Supreme according to the Word of God, your mind turned to the poor. Use this philosophical Work in this way, according to the canons or rules of Chymia, under the influence of nature, and rejoice in the Lord God.

Another Recipe

First, draw off its moisture and also wash it carefully and cleanly, sublimate it by itself without any addition, as long as something rises. Discard what is left over. Now sublimate it 6 or 7 times with as much quite clean and prepared common salt, put it on a glass plate in a damp cellar to dissolve it. Pour the dissolved matter back on it till everything is dissolved, or enclose it in a glass. Sublimate again with prepared salt what does not dissolve, and you have the Water of the Philosophical Mercury. Take as much of that as you like, and as much red, clean and pure Laton as it will absorb. Then put it in a closed urn and keep it for many days. You will see the Raven's Head in a short time, which will soon have white blossoms, then yellow, and finally red ones.

If you will be obedient to God, I will teach you how to make the Stone from two luminaries (as the old alchemists and their successors themselves made with their hands), without covert words, including the manipulation and its powers, its nature and first essence or substance. For one cannot deprive it of is effect, which nature has put into it or God in his outermost work, and it is done solely in these two lights.

Even if the two lights were lying till Doomsday in the chaos out of which they have come, Nature could not effect this with them, because Nature had infused her outermost power into them. That is why we will immediately bring these two lights out of their nature, a bad nature and form, into a better one. Therefore we must go backwards and separate what was together, what Nature had done, and bring it back into the form it was when Nature first began to act. To bring it into such a form, we must, as far as possible, follow Nature with the Art. Sometimes we must go beyond Nature by separating, rectifying, coagulating, purifying, combining, and incerating the earth, and undertake many other processes which Nature cannot do as she is not impelled to do such works. That is why the material has to be transformed into a better form than Nature has given it.

Then you must know how to draw off silver's incombustible sulfur, because silver is an imperfect body, cold, moist, and crude, containing much moisture and blackness. It is very earthly, crude, and feminine on account of its coldness. Therefore everybody piles silver upon gold. This is the reason why the combustible sulfur, the earthiness and blackness, has first to be removed from silver. So, take as much silver as you like, refine it on the cupel and laminate it. Then take the sublimated auripigment, the middle material, as has been taught in the work concerning it. Rind it small on a stone with vinegar to the consistency of a paste, coat the silver laminae, dry them in the sun, near a fire or in a room, put them in a crucible, one upon the other till the crucible is full, lute them together, put the matter for 12 hours in a calcinations furnace with a very small fire, so that the silver does not melt, cool it, pound it in an iron mortar or scrape the calcined matter off. If it is not yet calcined enough, calcine it again or till the silver is calcined, grind it on a stone with common distilled water, till the water again runs off clear from the powder. Then dry it in the sun or near the fire and preserve it in a glass. Evaporate the water with which the silver has been washed, refine the faeces on the cupel, and in this way you will not lose anything. File your silver finely, and Rx to one oz of silver take 3j of prepared arsenic. Stratify it, calcine it for 12 or 16 hours, then grind and wash it, as I taught before.

After this, take the silver powder, heat it to redness for 24 or 32 hours, then calcine it for 12 days in which the spirits are calcined, so that it lows red-hot ⁓ but not completely so. When the 12 days are over, let it glow modestly, brown, red, for 3 days, but so that it does not melt. Then cool it, and it is prepared.

For silver has two sicknesses, like other imperfect metals, but its two sicknesses do not go to the inmost root as do those of the other imperfect metals. One sickness is the combustible sulphur, the other is cold and humidity. The first sickness is eliminated with arsenic and washing. Know that the substance of arsenic is so strong that it burns and destroys all bodies. The same is done by auripigment and sulfur; these they are of one nature. Follow Nature with the Art. Sometimes we must go beyond Nature by separating, rectifying, dissolving, coagulating, purifying, combining, and incerating the earth, and undertake many other processes which nature cannot do, as she is not impelled to do such works. That is why the material has to be transformed into a better form than nature has given it.

Then you must know how to draw off silver's combustible sulfur, because silver is an imperfect body, cold, moist, and coarse, containing much moisture and blackness. It is very earthy, coarse, and feminine on account of its coldness. Therefore everybody piles silver upon gold. This is the reason why the combustible sulfur, the earthiness and blackness have first to be removed from silver. So, take as much silver as you like, refine it on the cupel and laminate it. Then take the sublimated auripigment, the middle material, as has been taught in the work concerning it, grind it small on a stone with vinegar, to the consistency of a paste, coat the silver laminae, dry them in the sun, near the fire, or in a room, put them in a crucible, one upon the other till the crucible is full, lute them together, put the substance for 12 hours in a calcination furnace with a very small fire, so that the silver does not melt. Cool it, pound it in an iron mortar or scrape the cacined matter off, and if it is not yet calcined enough, calcine it again until the silver is calcined. Now grind it on a stone with common water, then wash its blackness off in a lass dish with common distilled water, till the water again runs off clear from the powder. Then dry it in the sun or near the fire and preserve it in a glass. Evaporate the water with which silver has been washed, refine the faeces on the cupel, and in this way you will not lose anything. File your silver small, and Rx to 1 oz of silver, 3j of prepared arsenic; stratify it, calcine it for 12 or 16 hours, then grind and wash it, as I taught before.

After this, take the silver powder, heat it to redness for 24 or 32 hours, then calcine it for 12 days in the furnace in which the spirits are calcined, so that it glows red-hot, but not completely so. When the 12 days are over, let it glow modestly for 3 days, brown, red, but so that it does not melt, and it is prepared.

For silver has two sicknesses, like other imperfect metals, but its two sicknesses do not go to the innermost root as do those of the other imperfect metals. One sickness is the combustible sulfur, the other is cold and humidity. The first sickness is eliminated by arsenic and washing. Know that the substance of arsenic is so coarse that it burns and destroys all bodies. The same is done by auripigment and sulfur. These three are of one nature.

When arsenic and auripigment are disembodied and cleansed of their impurity, density, and wild unfixed spirits, and you take the middle spirit, then with this spirit you will draw away the combustibility of the sulfur of metals by calcining, washing, purging, reiterating. For if the poison in the theriac is not prepared, it will kill men; but when it is prepared, it drives the poison out. Likewise arsenic and auripigment.

Prepare the gold into a most subtle powder, as has been taught in the work on silver, in the following way: Rx, gold and silver prepared, mix them together, rubbing them on a stone with water like painters' color. Dry it again, reverbarate it on a big cupel, till it swells like a sponge, cool it, take it out, dissolve it in vinegar, distill it in the Balneum, as is said in the work on silver. Then dissolve it again, and continue doing this dissolving and coagulating till no more faeces are left. Now the Work is done about which Dantin says: Open the enclosed, wet it; close what has been opened, and dry it; do likewise with the coldness of Luna, and you will find the warmth of gold, and you will find the coldness of Luna.

Now the material is ready for extracting the Stone. Most of the material of the gold will rise and take with it all the subtle parts of silver. The parts of silver that are coarse, phlegmatic, and feminine remain at the bottom.

Sol alone is subtle and masculine in its parts. When Sol is dissolved and opened, it grows up altogether because of its great subtlety, but Luna stays at the bottom and is not yet ready to grow up on account of its coarseness.

There is therefore a contrary in these two lights; what is the ruin of one is the enhancement of the other, and that is why they belong together in the Work, as you well know.

After this, sublimate this material in the manner taught in the White and the Red. Watch out for the air when you open the glass, so that it does not kill you [Arsine, arsenic hydride].

For this reason allow the vessel to cool down completely. If the spirits went out through the lute during sublimation, or if the head were to break, or the glass or the pot, it would kill you by its subtle poison.

For there is no subtler or hotter, no more violent spirit among all metals than the spirit of Sol. If it were to open in its parts as is Luna or other metals, or if the 4 Elements that are together in Sol were contraries, it would sooner fly from the fire than from some other mineral spirits. But in Sol the Elements are all equal and tempered, and so clean that they are never separated.

Therefore, when Sol is opened, it flies together with others without leaving anything behind, unless something of other metals or baser things were intermixed with it, as there are many who melt other metallic bodies or minerals together with Sol, because everything that comes from minerals likes to dwell with gold and stays with it in a friendly manner, because Sol is the king and master. That is why anyone wishing to make a work with Sol alone must take care not to open Sol so much that the ferment follows it, otherwise one would rise with the other. If that happens, you must add some Sol to the ferment of fresh powder ∼ if you wish to make the Stone, but it would not serve anything to add red ferment. If it should happen that your Sol were to glow up immediately, it would be better for you to make the White Stone by using Luna. Melt the matter so that you can increase it with the spirit of Sol, and you will doubly benefit.

For you must make the White Stone by the power of Sol, and you must bring your spirit together with the soul, in her own might, of which instruction will be given in other works. You might ask: I believed that Sol had been fixed from the beginning, as it stays on the cupel, also in cement, in antimony, and in the fire ~ and if it stayed there flowing till Doomsday, it would not be burnt up. And if it were lying in the earth till the end of the world, would it be corrupted? Sol cannot be corrupted by anything in the world. Sol is simple, that is, in all its parts and Elements are not contraries, and its oil and salt are so united with the 4 Elements, and its Mercury and Sulfur are within so closely intermixed and in such proportion that they are one mature. They are equal in all their parts, so that Sol is nothing but one single thing, and one thing alone, which is not constituted of any other thing. You cannot separate it by anything. Therefore, Sol and Luna are opposed to air.

In regard to the Stone, when you sublimate, bind two glass eyemirrors in front of your eyes and a broad leather over your mouth and nose, into which leather a broad double woolen cloth must be sewn. On the broad cloth put a white sponge with which to tie up your nostrils and mouth. Protect yourselves thus from the air, because Sol and Luna rise invisibly, and the Stone is sublimated till it leaves no more faeces but is as beautiful and white as snow and clear as crystal.

You have now prepared Mercury, and the Sulfur of the Philosophers in all its power and subtlety. Keep all the faeces that have been left behind during sublimation, because you must reverberate them again. For it is the body of Luna that has not yet glowed up. You are to dissolve the body and the ferment of our Stone in the following way; the body out of the faeces with distilled vinegar ~ everything that will dissolve. Then coagulate it, after that reverberate it for 24 hours with a gentle fire, so that it does not get more than red-hot. Let it cool.

Now remove and dissolve it again with distilled vinegar, coagulate it, reverbarate it for 5 or 6 hours, not letting it become more than red-hot. Allow it to cool, dissolve it again with common water, coagulate it again. Thereafter heat it to a red heat for the duration of 5 or 6 Pater Nosters. Now take it out again and dissolve it in common water until nothing is left behind. If that is not the case, dissolve and coagulate it again till almost all the moisture is evaporated and distilled, then let it cool. When it is cold, should be together, pieces as large as a finger's length, clear as crystal and white as snow.

This manipulation must be done in glass bowls made for the purpose, standing in a boiling Balneum, and the cask must be covered with a double linen cloth to prevent any dust or impurity from falling into it. Our work must be clean, clean in the extreme, when you prepare your Pretiosa terra and your Corpus, and you prepare the Soul to receive and absorb your ferment in great unity and peace, so that they will nevermore be separated from each other but shall at all times reign with great subtlety and powers.

The Body desires to receive its own Soul and Spirit, while the Soul with the Spirit desire to come down and rest with their own Body, because one cannot be without the other. When they are then together, one in the other as they are supposed to be, held by an immovable and unchangeable button, one nature, one simple thing like the invincible heaven ~ then it is the Fifth Essence by which all diseases can be cured and resolved.

There are many ways to make the Stone, but one is more difficult, laborious, and longer than the other, and not all are equally high in the projection. The Stone made with the great ferment is less potent than one made with a prepared body. Consequently, you must make projection after a subtle Work. The Stone must be extracted from Sol and Luna. Both must be Rebus vir. (Aleph), the Red man and the Alba Foemina, the White Woman, if a right union is to occur; because the hot Red Man must act upon the cold White Woman, if you wish to obtain fruit from the union, and a perfect Work is to take place.

For you would be unable to separate anything from a pure simple thing, just as pure water does not turn into anything but pure water, although it may be purified if it contains faeces. You can extract and purify those by various manipulations, and this water is then better than the first, but it remains water, and you cannot make anything else from it.

Thus it is with Sol and Luna if you try to work with each one separately. Sol is Sol and remains Sol. Luna is Luna and remains so, unless you spiritualize it and add it to its own body in order to congeal its own spirit, so as to enable it to make projection upon purified metals in the 3rd Order. It is a simple medicine of the 3rd Order and nothing else.

The Stone must be made from spiritual things that cannot be separated, and from two natures, cold and hot, from snow and light, white and red, gross and subtle, man and woman, so that one acts upon the nature of the other, making the gross subtle, and the subtle gross; the light heavy, the hot cold, the moist dry, and the dry moist. Thus one nature acts upon another until finally all things are turned into one simple nature. Then each thing will be in a better condition and in a better higher form, or also in another substance, then the thing is perfect like an invincible heaven, which is simple. But the earth does not require any moisture, which is given it in abundance by heaven. Likewise with heat and cold.

Everything the earth lacks, heaven can supply in abundance. Nevertheless, heaven is neither cold nor warm, neither moist nor dry, a simple body and perfect in the extreme perfection and quality. Consequently, everything the earth, plants, trees, human beings, and animals requires, is supplied by heaven in abundance. Likewise with heat and cold, and everything else needed by the earth. Heaven can give it abundantly owing to the great powers with which God has invested it by His divine ordination and wonderful omnipotence.

Thus you are to understand that the Stone is a simple medicine of the 3rd Order, because our Stone must have the property which God has invisibly instilled into heaven. Therefore we must infuse into it the same quality of our Philosophical mastery, so that it may have the same quality and mastery that exists in a simple body — and when it has all this quality and power, only then is it our Stone.

In this way I have taught you how and out of what the Stone is to be made and of what quality it must be before it can be called the Stone.

Now take the body or the earth or the ferment, weigh it, and write it in a book. Put it in such a glass as is illustrated here. Then take 8 parts of ferment, 3 of your sublimation and put it in a small glass. Pour distilled water on the ferment, put on each glass some cut glass fitted to the mouth of the glass, set each in hot Balneum, and it will at once dissolve into clear water. When they are dissolved, pour both water together into a glass, stir well ~ they mingle easily ~ because they wish to be friends. The man wants his own lady of the house; the lady of the house, her own man; the dry cold earth wants the moisture of the water. Thus one wants to embrace the other and to enter into the other to the inmost root. There is then a perfect mingling ~ and yet it is not a perfect mingling, as when there is water mingling with water there is no hindrance, it is done immediately without any delay, for each desires to receive the other on account of the great purity which both have, and one loves the other.

Thus one penetrated the other in the first mingling which took place in clear water. Mix the clear water one with the other, as has been said above, distill it in the Balneum with the receptacle and the alembic well luted, draw the moisture off to dry it to a powder, take it out and congeal it in the secret furnace, as is taught in the White Work. Heat it in the same way, and in a short time you will see that all the material has become black. Then you will know what a perfect union has occurred, and underneath the blackness the whiteness is concealed. If the blackness does not appear in the Work, no perfect union will take place, or fixation between Soul, Spirit, and Body. It holds that together which is the means, the Salt of the Wise, which keeps the Soul, the Body, and the Spirit alive, causing one to enter the other. The salt is still lying in the inmost of the body, because the spirit has not drawn the soul out of the body, where the Salt of nature remains hidden in the deepest of the mixture.

The salt is the medium which keeps spirit, body, and soul together, and the salt lies buried in the deepest of the mixture. How then can the salt be shared with them when it is not drawn out of the deepest of the mixture together with the spirit which would rise along with it? How then could the salt be part of the spirit? The salt has within itself a soul, and that is why it is a medium between body, soul, and spirit, because it must share in them, must keep spirit, soul, and body together with its sharpness, so that one may permeate the other.

If the salt is not extracted from the body by the spirit, carrying the soul in it as it rises, it remains hidden in the deepest of the body. Consequently, the salt must be extracted fro the body with the spirit, containing a soul and a spirit. Together with those it must rise and become one thing with them, if it is to be a medium between the spirit and the body, because the salt contains a soul and a body. It cannot live without a soul belonging to it, and the soul cannot be without the spirit. Therefore the salt must be one thing with the spirit, and the spirit with the soul. That is why the salt is a medium between these two, if they wish to remain together.

Arnoldus de Villanova says that the salt is wonderful, and from these words it is evident that no perfect fixation can be accomplished if the salt is not extracted from the body with the spirit, as is prescribed. They fail each time who make an amalgam with Sol and [?], or with Luna, and Mercury, and try to fix them. It cannot be done at all, because the salt lies in the deepest of Sol and Luna, and it cannot be extracted from the inmost of Sol and Luna by any substance in the world except by their own spirit ~ and not by any foreign spirits.

Sol and Luna must therefore be opened and freed in such a way that they let go of their spirit, thus drawing the salt, and with it the soul from the deepest of Sol and Luna, and carrying them upward into heaven, to become one nature with it.

When now body and spirit are prepared with the slat which carries the soul in it, when the soul is purified and reunited with its own purified body, spirit, and slat, there will be a right conjunction, and the whole will become black. Where this is done, blackness should appear. Therefore it is obvious that all amalgamations, fixations, cinnabars, or all other crazy, enticing, fast works are wrong and deceitful (although they appear to be something). You should avoid all of them with their false opinions, and take great care to be enlightened by the philosophy according to the ancients who say on their books that our stone, which is to b extracted, must be made out of one things only and not out of many, nor must anything be added to it, be it small or big. But extract its soul and discard from it everything superfluous, purify its body, add that again to its soul, and it will live forever.

When you see its blackness, you will be sure that its conjunction has taken place. After that, continue with the fire from one degree to another, be it of whatever color it may, as is taught in the White Work. When you see that, remove it, mix it, and test it on a glowing sheet to see if it is fixed and can stand fire. Then take it out and calcine it in the reverbaration furnace for 24 hours with a gentle fire. Let it cool, weigh it, then dissolve it as prescribed. When both are dissolved in clear water, mix them together as said before, draw the moisture off in the Balneum, and congeal it in the secret furnace as before.

Note here that it is not necessary to dissolve the spirit. The Stone gets stronger in every solution and coagulation, and it becomes a hundred times more powerful in projection. It is also the surest ferment for dissolving the spirits, both in clear water. Therefore they must be mixed together dry, because that is a better and surer mixture than mingling water with water, as said above. When the spirit has been fixed with the ferment, it has also to be calcined and coagulated to make the Work as subtle as possible, so that another projection can be made with it afterwards.

Take 4 parts of ferment and 1 part of spirit, mix them. But you must not calcine, dissolve, and coagulate often. The Work would far too soon begin to melt under your hands, so that no calcinations could be done. Therefore, if you wish to make an important Work, and a very subtle one, take much ferment and little spirit. Then you can calcine, dissolve, and coagulate the Work frequently. Whether you add mush or little spirit to the ferment, it takes an equally long time. If you add but a little spirit to the ferment, the Work is fixed. If you add much spirit to the ferment, it will take longer till it begins to congeal. After that, do as prescribed. Take 1 part of spirit to 8 parts of ferment, dissolve, and mix them together, as said above, till the material becomes as liquid that it can no longer be made red-hot or calcined. Then stop and give the spirit in the right amount. When that is done, continue increasing the fire from degree to degree till, with God's help and praise, you reach the perfect redness.

Multiplication

Multiplication means multiplying your Stone in its power but not in its size, that is, it should increase in its nobility and subtlety, so that, if it now does 10,000 in the projection, its projection will reach 100,000 after it has been multiplied, subtilized, and elevated in its greatness and power.

If you multiply and subtilize the Stone 3 times in its power, its projection will be without end because of its great subtlety, so that it could be multiplied so often that the end of the projection could never be reached.

But it might also be multiplied so often that it could not be kept in any glass. It would go through it, and if you wished to dissolve it, it would go through the glass invisibly. The glass would not be broken, but its color would be changed into that of a ruby. So, when the Stone has been made, set the glass to melt, throw the Stone on it, as much powder as you care to take as if you wished to transmute tin into Sol. When the Stone is melted, the glass will have the color of a ruby. Now set the glass to melt and keep it molten in the crucible for a half hour, and your material will become so hard that it will never again melt. And in that hard state it will have as wonderful colors as very beautiful spotless rubies.

The ancients said that the glass thus made by the Stone is much more precious than natural rubies, of which you will read in the Book of Stones, written by Hermes. Because Hermes says: If your Stone is thrown on anything that can be melted and which is not metal but a thing of Nature, it will change it into itself, as much as it is able to do, just as God created man like him in regard to eternity, liberty, and many other things too long to enumerate. The Stone converts a thing into itself, and it will be a thing of one nature. In the world nothing is found that is One nature, except crystals, glass, or precious stones. All other things are made of composed things, they are not made of One thing. From crystals or glass nothing can result but crystals or glass, though it is possible to infuse color into them, whichever you like. On white crystal glass, which is like a fine smooth plate, you can write whatever you wish. Likewise the Stone; it adds wonderful colors to crystals or glass, and it makes its like in the colors, though not in the same degree and power that it would be converted into them and make projection with them. But it is very wonderful and beautiful and the finest in the world, also much more precious than gold. The glass never melts or burns.

Therefore, when the crystals or glass are melted in a strong crucible, throw the Stone on them till you see that you like the color, because the Stone penetrates glass or crystal like oil does strong leather. When the color pleases you, stop throwing more of the Stone on it and let the crystals burn together with the Stone till the material develops into a King and becomes hard and transparent, because the [Symbol (-|)] converts all fusible things into undissolvable ones, and all undissolvable ones into fusible ones, it makes all hard bodies tender, and all tender bodies hard, and all combustible things incombustible. But it (the King) does not have this property. Therefore it cannot be called a Stone, because it is no more than a medicine of the second Order, and nothing but the invincible heaven. For what the earth lacks, heaven can supply, and yet, what it gives is not of its nature. Likewise our Stone: It makes all dry bodies moist and all moisture dry, all coldness hot and al heat cold, all impurities pure, and unspeakably more of the same.

If you wish to make such rubies, do as is prescribed. When they have cooled, cut them into pieces and smooth them in a stone mill at your discretion. Thus you will have the very finest rubies without spots. They will rejoice men's hearts and render a master who wears them victorious and cause him to dominate his enemies. He is loved by men and protected from disease. That is why you must multiply the Stone so often that it becomes quite subtle. But if you wish to dissolve it in the red burning water to make it go invisibly through the glasses, you will be deprived of your stone, and finally you will be unable to keep it in the glasses, even if they were 10 feet thick.

Therefore, multiply your Stone in the following manner: prepare an AF of vitriol, clarified and purified of its faeces, and as much Salt. Distill it according to the Art. Then take the Death's Head, pulverize it finely, pour common distilled water over it. Let the salt leach, dissolve, and sink. Filter it till it is clear, coagulate it again. When it is coagulated, pulverize it again, put it in a large glass pot, pour into it the distilled AF, and distill again whatever can be distilled. Now take the Death's Head, pulverize it as before, and continue this manipulation till you have distilled all the salt with the AF Then you have a precious red water, shining at night like fire and lightning.

Now rectify your water several times in the Balneum with pouring of and pouring on, till you have at last distilled everything over. Thus a wonderful water is prepared, in which you must multiply and open your Stone. Take your blessed Stone, dissolve it in this water, it will dissolve immediately. Put it in a lukewarm Balneum, the alembic and the receptacle firmly luted all around, and keep it warm.

When now your AF has been distilled over, take a little of the powder in the glass pot, put it on a red-hot plate, and see if it smokes, as I have taught elsewhere. Pour the water back on it, lute it again, distill as before till there is nothing left to distill. Then try and test it again as before, to see if it now smokes somewhat.

If it does not smoke more than the first time, pour AF on it again, set it in the Balneum and do as has been taught before. Continue with this manipulation till everything smokes off the red-hot plates. Then it is opened and dissolved enough. Now sublimate it 3 or 4 times as before, each time without adding anything, as it requires no faeces, then it is enough.

Now take a small part of the sublimated substance, and in order to congeal the material, set it in a retort-glass in the furnace in which the spirits are calcined, put a small piece of glass on its mouth, give it first a small fire or heat, increasing the fire all the time by degrees, as is taught in the Work. When it is fixed, weigh it to see how much there is of the fixed part. Then take 1 part of the spirit to 3 parts of the fixed material, set it again to congeal, as taught before, and do this till everything sublimated is fixed. It will be congealed immediately. When it is quite fixed in all its parts, the other parts which had been added to the first part, will be less fixed than the first, because one part fixes the other part.

In this multiplication there will be no blackness, and no colors whatsoever will appear, nor whiteness. Even during sublimation nothing else appears but the redness, because the Stone has no other color than red, for it is nothing but a sublimation, invincible like the simple heaven, a simple clarified body. For it must be one only if it is to make projection, spirit, soul, and body equally strong. If the body were stronger than the spirit, or the spirit stronger than the body, its nature would be made of opposites which would not be one thing only. Nevertheless, it would not have been brought out of its own nature into another nature, yet that is how it must be. If it were not so, it would not accomplish any projection. The Stone must be sublimated, thereby changing it from a fixed nature into a spiritual one. Our body is a body, soul, and spirit, and these three are one thing only, joined together indivisibly, one great power, on substance, and one nature. In their being on, they are like the Holy Trinity. Father, Son and Holy Ghost, three in One in the might, and One in the simple of the substance, and one is not without the other. The Father is not the Son, the Son is not the Holy Ghost, nor is the Holy Ghost the Father, and yet these three Persons are eternally one simple substance.

And thus our Stone is neither fixed nor volatile. It is both, body and spirit, and both must be equally strong in its nature, as it is taught. It seems to be fixed enough to stand the fire. This is due to its firm inter-penetration; the parts of the Stone have inter-penetrated so strongly that it is quite compact, and in addition there is in the world nothing cleaner and subtler. The cleaner and subtler a thing is, the more the clean and subtle things are firmly combined and inter-penetrated, and the heavier their weight is. For they love each other, so that they are merged into one and can hardly be separated from one another. See how it can stand the fire. The fire cannot overcome its parts because they are so firm. Nevertheless it is a pure spirit, because now that it is open, it flies away much more easily than some spirits. This is so on account of its great subtlety, its great cleanliness, both of which belong to its nature.

How could our Stone not fight fire better and more strongly? For it is both, composed of body and spirit. As they are both one, how could the Stone not resist fire more strongly and mightily than gold, and it also resists fire. Our Stone must therefore resist fire a thousand times more strongly than Sol.

When now our Stone is open and unlocked by our burning water which separates its condensed parts, and swells like a sponge, Sol flies up with a small fire, smaller than that required for some spirits, due to the great subtlety that God has bestowed on it. How much sooner then will our Stone fly up than Sol, with little heat and less fire, because our Stone has the extreme subtlety and power that can be given it, so that it is a thousand times subtler than Sol. When then its parts are united in the right proportion, so that they inter-penetrate, we call it fixed.

Thus the Stone must again pass through the fire and suffer what it suffered before, and a thousand times more, when it will become a thousand times and more subtle than before. For as often as you open and close the Stone, make it subtle and sublimate it, and again unite it, as often it obtains a stronger nature and tinges a thousand times more than before. If you multiply the Stone, elevate or exalt it in its potency, its nature is not changed, because it does not become black, nor does it produce various colors, but it remains in is own essence and nature, the same which it had in the beginning. When it has been processed to the extreme, so that no manipulation or art in the world can change it from its simple substance, you can nevertheless make it subtler still, also open and close as it as prescribed, subtilize it and open it in small parts, so that its parts may be made firmer, all the more. We call that fixation, and it is nothing but making firm, so that all subtle parts may be better be kept together than before, to enable us to make projection with it. Thus the Stone may be multiplied three or four times, but no more, as it would become far too subtle and would disappear invisibly.

Thus the ancients used to make the Stone, as have been taught above, before the art of the strong water had been invented. Then the lights had to be dissolved, slowly by hand, with calcinations, reverberation, and dissolution in our strong acetum distillatum and with coagulating till our Stone was spiritual. After that, they worked as has been taught before. And when the Stone was completed, they did not know the right art to multiply it in its own power. They only had one single Stone. After its projection they worked to make it subtle by dissolving it in strong acetum destillatum, then coagulated it till it turned into a fine oil. When they wished to turn the oil back into a hard mass, they took one part of gold, disembodies it and make it red like blood. They mixed it together with their dissolve oil, coagulated it and put it in the secret furnace in moderate heat till it was changed into a dark mass, red like dragon's blood, which was now subtler than before on account of its many dissolutions and coagulations.

All this their successors saw. They sharpened their wits and discovered strong water, whereby they shortened the long way. For they made AF with which they could rub both bodies inside, and after the purification they mixed the water, worked the mixture without faeces till it was transparent and clear, and thus managed easily to bring it to spirituality and its extreme perfection. With the same strong water well rectified, they could subtilize and multiply the Stone in its own power and that in every way, as said before. The AF is a great aid for shortening the Work and achieving a higher projection of the Stone, with the help of God.

In addition, I will teach you how to infuse the spirit of the Red Man into the body of the White Woman. It is a pleasant and noble thing and work of the Art, as you will hear.

Therefore, take first silver, cleanly refined on the cupel and purified of Saturn. Dissolve it in its white Water, pushs it to the bottom, wash it carefully of its salt in warm water, reverbarate it so that it swells, then dissolve in rectified distilled vinegar, all that will dissolve. Reverbarate the rest again, and dissolve it as before, till everything is dissolved. Thereafter draw the vinegar off and dissolve everything that will dissolve in common rectified water. Gather all these solutions. Dry what does not dissolve, then dissolve it again in distilled vinegar, and if it still does not dissolve, reverbarate it once more, so that it may dissolve more easily in vinegar. If it were to dissolve better in water, it would be fine. Let it stand thus and dissolve it in distilled vinegar. Draw the vinegar off and dissolve it in common water. Continue doing this till everything is dissolved into clear water. Now draw this off, calcine the Luna somewhat to remove the spirit of vinegar from it. Thereafter, dissolve it again in common water. If there were anything that does not dissolve, clean it again or prepare it wit the solution of the vinegar. Then calcine it till everything is dissolved in water, without faeces and spirit of vinegar. Then draw the water off dry, and your Luna thus purified is quite suitable for this Work. Keep this white body in a glass jar, in a warm room, to keep it dry.

Thereafter take Sol, well purified in Regal Cement, dissolve it in its red water, put it in some rectified common water, wash the lime carefully of the salt of the aforesaid water, dry it, and set it to be calcined in the vaulted furnace in order to open it, for 12 days, in mild heat. Then put it into is rectified water, dissolve it in the Balneum, and leave it standing in it to putrefy for 83 days. Then distill the water off and put what is left at the bottom of a glass crucible, wit a piece of cut glass over its mouth. Set this in a receptacle cut through the middle, put the upper part back, set an alembic with a receptacle luted to it in sand or ashes, standing so deep that the material is two or three fingers' breadth in the ashes. First give a small fire, then gradually a stronger, till the big receptacle turns visibly rd-hot. Keep it standing in hat heat for 8 days, then let it cool of its own, and take it out.

If it is still whole, leave the Sol in it, but if it is broken up, put it in another glass inside a strong earthenware cask, so that two crucibles are adjusted to each other. Put your glass inside, well luted, likewise the crucible well luted one on top of the other. First let it dry, then calcine more and more till the earthenware cask is red-hot, but take care that the Sol does not melt. Let it stand in this heat for 12 days, then let it cool of itself, remove your Sol, and you will find it red like dragon's blood.

And this is a sign that it has been dismembered. If it were not red, rather yellow or in between, it would have to be dissolved again in its red rectified water. Then proceed as taught here. Therefore continue till it is dismembered and red like blood. Then put what is red in the rectified water till it is completely putrefied and everything has become volatile at the same time. Now push it to the bottom, wash its salt off neatly, dissolve it in distilled vinegar and in common rectified water, coagulate and calcine it gently in the calcination furnace for spirits, so as to remove from it the spirit of vinegar but not to lose any of its natural moisture.

Now sublimate it according to the Art, as said elsewhere, and continue with this sublimation till nothing is left behind. Then the spirit is well prepared or purified. Use it to increate the body of Luna till it reaches perfect whiteness. Thereafter bring it to redness, as taught before.

If you wish to multiply its might and power, and if it has previously been turned into the White and the Red, enough work has been done. Use your Stone in the peace and obedience of God.

This Is The Book of the Stone
And Its Subsequent Projection

Now I must and will teach you how you are to use the Stone. If you intend to convert the Stone into Sol and Luna, do not throw it on anything unless it has first been prepared to this end. If you wish to throw it on tin, melt it in a crucible to test it with 1 lb of tin and 3/3 fine silver together. Throw your White Stone on it, and this tin will be transformed into genuine silver, much or less according to the subtlety of the Stone, as you will hear later. If you wish to throw your red Stone, throw it on silver. It is not necessary to open the latter. All you have to do is melt it and throw a Red Stone on it, and Luna will turn into genuine Sol, better than that which comes out of the mines.

Always throw your White Stone on tin, and not on other metals, because the Stone must do nothing but cook it completely, as I have taught elsewhere. The other metals might also be converted into silver, but they are much impurer than tin, and the projection would not be as high. In addition, the Stone would have to be worked much longer in the fire together with the impure metals before it would result in a King. That is why the Stone has to be thrown on tin, because tin is closest to Luna.

After that, make a projection of the Red Stone on Luna, because Luna is the purest and cleanest metal on which you can make projection. Nor can any projection with the Red Stone be made except on Luna alone. If you throw the Red Stone on lead or another metal, it will not accomplish anything, as the red Stone makes nothing but gold, and no metal results in gold unless they are first tuned into silver. For gold has always first been silver before it becomes gold.

Nature must first produce silver before the latter turns into gold, because one cannot get beyond 100 miles unless one has walked the way that lies between.

But throw the White Stone on whatever metal you wish, it till turn silver. It happens because you are making your metals come alive and infuse your soul into them, as Morienus says: Our metal is not a vulgar metal, for it is alive and has a soul.

For one cannot reach the third degree from the first, as is taught in vegetabili, animalu and minerali. One has to know the manner of projection. If you throw the Stone on silver or tin, you will not accomplish anything. Even if you had already infused a soul into the metals, or if it were a living body such as silver, the Stone must be admixed nevertheless. If it had penetrated quite subtly and firmly, and even if it were a powder and the metal were roughly melted, it would stand nonetheless on top of the metals upon which it is thrown. When then it stands on the metals, the Stone may well melt and float on the metal, spreading above, but it will keep the metal from moving. It protects it to prevent the combustible sulfur from flying away, and the fire from consuming the metal, because the Stone lies on it like oil.

However, it does not mix with the metals, as little as oil mixes with water if the two are brought together, but instead it stays still. Thus oil always floats on top, preserving the water from foreign moisture, so that the latter cannot enter the water, and the water or the subtle spirit does not evaporate because of the air, as all waters have a subtle spirit.

For if you let your water stand 4 or 5 days, as it is, uncovered, it will soon smell bad, being robbed of its subtle spirits. If the oil were to float on it, however, it would not smell bad even if it stood thus for 10 days. The oil protects the water from corruption and prevents its spirit from plying away.

How is it that oil does not mix with water and always floats on top of it, although it is heavier than water? You must know that oil has no part in the water, although it had been one body with the water. The Quinta Essentia contains the oil together with other things. When the oil is beaten, one sees very well that it is white. The Quinta Esentia has come from one thing only. Water, Fire, Air, Earth, Oil, and Salt, all kept together, must be separated because, just as the Quinta Essentia has come from one thing only, they must all separate from each other. Thereafter, they must no longer be combined before they are clarified. That is why Fire, that is the Oil, will not mingle, although it had formed one body with the water, although the oil contains a much coarser part. It also contains Sol. The parts of the oil are firmly interpenetrated, so that they do not separate from one another. It is a firm Element and quite open, due to the coarseness which it contains. The oil is subtle and fiery and firmly presses into one, so that all the fieriness will be above, and all subtlety will rise, and the firm parts do not wish to separate to enable them to penetrate through the firm water, on account of the evil smell, and that is why the oil must necessarily swim above.

Likewise our Stone. It also floats on the metals like oil on water, because the Stone does not form a part of the metals, although it had been a metal. However, it is heavier than metal, that is, it is subtle and stands on the molten metal as firmly as water.

Consequently, the Stone does not have the nature of metals, for it is only Quint.Ess,, that is why it will not intermix or interpenetrate, and this is due to its fatty parts, and it must needs swim above.

Hermes says that our Stone must form a part with Body, Soul, and Spirit. But in the Stone the parts are united in such a perfection and such a spiritual substance that they do not mix with the impure parts, except by a means which must be united with the spiritual substance, be it White or Red.

No conjunction can occur in any things that are contraries except by a means which causes the two extremities to penetrate and embrace each other and stay together. Likewise in the projection of the Stone. It does not wish to stay, mix with, and penetrate the rotten, evil smelling, black, imperfect metals without a means. For the impure black metals are contraries like the Stone and cannot be mixed together and penetrates without a means. This must be a living body, and the same living body must be one with the Stone, White or Red. When these two unclean evil-smelling metals have within themselves this unclean living body, which is one with them like the soul with the body, and the White or the Red Stone is thrown upon them, and they now also have within themselves the same living body, then they can be joined. Thus each begets its own of its own nature, so that a conjunction results and one penetrates the other. The Stone expels all their corruption and produces a perfect living body, better than those from the mines.

Now I will teach you how you must prepare the Stone, White or Red, so that it adapts to the crude metals and penetrates them. It is done as follows: Take the Red Stone, 1 part, and Sol 1000 parts. Beat it into thin sheets. Then take sulfur, pound it with a stone into a thick pap with olive oil, and grease your sheets with it, dry them, put them on hot coals and calcine them. Thereafter pulverize them and wash the powder off with common water till the water runs off the powder clear and pure. Pound the powder further on a stone with honey or gum-water, the way one pounds painters' paint. Then put it in a glass bowl and wash it again with common distilled water. The powder will sink to the bottom. Pour the water off and continue doing this till the water runs off clear from the powder. After this, dry it again in the sun or on a small fire, and your gold is ready.

Thereafter take 1000 parts of this powder and 1 part of the Stone pulverized finely, mix them together. Then take a crucible that can well stand a good strong fire. Upon this crucible set another crucible, like a closed dish. Grind both well on a stone to make them fit tightly, add your powder, lute the crucible inside and outside strongly and carefully, by 3 or 4 fingers' breadth, and dry the lute well. Then set it in another crucible in a wind-furnace, first with a small fire, then ever stronger and stronger, from degree to degree, till the crucible is red hot. Therefore increase your fire considerably till you are sure that the material is melting in the crucible. Therefore, let the crucible stand for 3 days in such a heat as will keep the material in fusion all the time. Then let it cool of its own, break the crucible open, and you will find a hard mass, brittle like glass, which can be pulverized. When you wish to make projection, take 1 part of this powder, 1000 parts of the pure metal insouled and made alive, transmute it into real Sol and Luna, better than the mineral. This is the Work of 3 Days of which the ancients wrote in their books, and it is the Work which renders the base bodies so subtle in 3 days that, if the Stone is thus melted, the gold becomes more medicinal than it was at first, always more so than is believable. This is a secret.

The Stone thus prepared does not make projection on mercury, because of its non-fusibility, as with this Stone no projection is made except to the Red on Luna and to the White on tin. Therefore, need be done except to make the Stone infusible. Enough has been said of this in the Multiplicaton, how to turn the Stone into Oil, and it is therefore not necessary to say anything about mercury.

If you wish to work with the oil, and wish to throw it on mercury, take 1 part of mercury, half an ounce of fine silver as it comes from the cupel, and amalgamate them, 1 lb of mercury for one amalgam. Put this in a glass crucible, then in an earthenware crucible, set it thus in the fire, and when it begins to smoke, throw it on your prepared oil of the Stone, previously prepared and tested with the body in tripode as I have taught in the Multiplication.

And now I will teach you another way. Take some oil of the Red or the White Stone, and take Sol to the Red, so that 1 part of oil and 10 parts of Sol come together, as has already been taught before. Pour the oil into the calx Sol, set it in tripodem in a glass hanging lamp, first with s small fire, then somewhat stronger, so that you could hardly hold your hand in the inmost furnace, and keep it thus for 5 or 6 days.

Thereafter increase the fire for 3 days so much that the uppermost or exterior furnace hisses when touched with a wet finger. Then let it cool of its own, take it out, break the glass open, and you will find a hard mass If you wish to make a projection on mercury, put it in a crucible, take some of this mass, pulverize it and throw it. Then increase the fire so that your material begins to melt. Let it melt till it results in a King. Then take it out, let it cool, knock it with a hammer, see it if is supple, then you have accomplished it and you have good Sol.

And mark! As long as it is brittle like glass, it is still a medicine. After that, thro it on molten silver, till the silver is supple and sticks beneath the hammer, then you have good Sol. But as long as it is brittle, you have not yet reached the end of the projection, be it with the White or the red oil. Then you must throw it on other metal till it is supple and has beautiful colors, and can stand all tests. Now you are at the end of the projection. When the Stone has been made as it should, be it White or Red, as I have taught in the Multiplication, its projection is infinite, which is unbelievable, but one can hardly reach the end. But do not do anything except throw it more and more on metals as long as it remains supple and passes all tests, as I have taught.

The Red and the White Stones

And coagulate out of clean and white sulfur and out of clean mercury; therefore coagulate, if they are quite pure, because the Stone, when it is coagulated, consists of clean white sulfur and pure Mercury. It is therefore white arsenic, pure and subtle, and it is the purest of all combined things. When it consists of pure red sulfur, combined with shining arsenic, it is pure and much subtler than the white arsenic.

Example: If you gave of it 1 part to a horse, the horse would die because the poison would go to the heart and thereafter to all parts, so that all flesh and everything there is to the horse would turn to poison, which would cause it to die. If dogs or birds were to eat of this dead horse, they would also die, for if such poison can kill a horse, which weighs so many hundred pounds, all animals that eat this must die also.

Thus our Stone is made of the same things as arsenic, be it white or red. Nature has cooked it thus for a long time and has drawn out its innermost. She has turned the materia, which at first was a great poison, back into a crude medicine, because Sol not only serves as a cure for all diseases on account of its great balance, but also because of its intermixture with other substances.

Our Work is made of these two, Sol and Luna, as is customary in the Work. Take Sol and Luna and undo again what nature has accomplished, that is, what she has turned into a body in many years. Dissolve it and turn it back into the prima material, as it was when nature first began to operate. It will again become arsenic and poison. When it is then extracted by subtle manipulation and mastery, the matter will become more poisonous than it was before Nature began to act. If you were to give one lot of this material to a horse or an ox, they would soon die, because the material is now so subtle and so very poisonous and hot that it is inexpressible. Thereafter, the material is sublimated and becomes quite thick, so that the fumes would unexpectedly kill a man. If you were to put some of this material on a chair and a an were to sit on it for the duration of 4 or 5 Pater Nosters, the material would penetrate the man's body, causing him to die soon. Nor does there exist such a strong animal in the world, even if it were a big poisonous dragon, that would not die at once if the fumes touched its body.

That is why the ancients likened the material to a poisonous dragon, saying that the dragon had eaten its own tail. They also called this material a snake, and compared it to a snake that impregnates itself. They used many other names for it which are too many to write about, all they meant was the Stone.

Therefore, no poison is found anywhere as strong as this material of the Stone, because of its subtlety, the heat which it has when it is sublimated. Then the master with his Philosophical Art causes the poison to be turned back inward into the innermost of its body. After that, the material possesses a great medicinal power which lies hidden in its innermost. It is that which the Master has brought to light by his Art, with the help of God.

When this has been done, its innermost has been brought outside, and what was outside has gone inside. Understand this also of the horse of which I have spoken. Such a Stone can do an infinite projection when it has been brought into its heavenly nature. For if a thing is good outside, it an do

1,000,000 times more than one that is bad outside. Example: The Lord God is good outside, the devil bad outside. Who then has more power, God or the devil? Likewise with our Stone. When it was still poisonous, how many big animals may it have killed? But after it is made good, how much good will it do? With its small weight it can always do a thousand times better, and more than 10, 20, thousand times better than Luna, it would seem impossible.

Under the green crudeness the blackness lies hidden, and every created thing has its perfect redness, either white in its innermost or in its exterior, and between the white and the red there are varied colors, more than one can imagine. But that which is white on the outside is red within, and between the two there are many kinds of colors, as said before. The closer a thing is to is perfection, the fewer colors it has within; and the simpler it is, the closer it is to its ultimate destination which God has assigned to it. Then it has no more than one color within it, neither more in its exterior nor in its interior, but it contains the power of all the colors which at first manifested within it. For as many colors as are in a thing, and as much variety there is within it, as many powers it contains, When the thing has been prepared into a simple perfected substance, in the uttermost power assigned to it by God, all these powers act together, like one thing, in a short time, nevertheless miraculously.

There is nothing else in things but a simple essence, and its body is red, and its interior is outside, and there is no difference in its middle. Just as it is in its middle, it is in its outside and also in its middle. Each does its work without ill humor, so to speak, in one moment. For there is no contrary nature within it which would act against it. It therefore acts promptly. Likewise our Stone. Wherever it is thrown, a perfect work is achieved, and in everything it turns the outer inside, and the inside outside.

Inside Luna is good, Sol is clear red, and when the White Stone is thrown on mercury, it draws the inmost outside, which turns into white clear silver, replacing the redness inside. Thus every single thing contains its tincture, be it white or red, although the Red and the White Stone have no nature which they could impart, just as it does not happen with the nature of stones. They do not have it in themselves to do violence, be it white or red, for God has given each thing its necessaries of life, and each thing contains enough tincture without necessitating the help of anything else. And each thing, be it vegetable or animal, contains its own medicine, without having to add another thing, to enable it to recover of itself. If it were not so, God's Work would not be perfect. All the things He has created have never lacked anything. They do not require help from other things, as they have in themselves everything they need, although we do not understand this completely. God has not forgotten anything in anything He has created. Nor is anything lacking in any leaf that grows out of the earth, although we do not perceive the perfection which is contained therein. But by the mastery of this Art we can draw out of each thing its occult nature and make manifest what is hidden in it, and hide what is manifest. That is what our Stone does in the white and red metals.

In the perfection of the red and white metals the Stone has no tincture, because the tincture which thus unites the Stone is with the Elements, so that there is one body and one substance which cannot be separated. For this is a heavenly nature, like the invincible heaven where all planets are sanding, Each according to its nature takes its influence from it and imparts to the things of the lower world, as we can daily see with our eyes, through the forces of the sun. Flowers grow in many different colors and varied fragrances, and all this is due to the warmth of the sun.

Do you believe that the world bestows color and fragrance to flowers and plants from its own body? No, not at all, but it is a heavenly nature that possesses so much power and influence that it draws out color, smell, and taste of the seed from which plants and flowers grow. Therefore. Although the sun were shining for a hundred years, it would not infuse either color, smell, or taste, but God has poured them into the seed. All this is locked inside the seed, and even if the sun were never to shine upon it, it would nevertheless get color, small, and taste. The sun is a heavenly body and it has the power to draw out by its heat and innermost in the seed and to manifest it on the outside; smell, taste, and color. The seed grows into its perfection, and it may thereafter grow superabundantly to the end of the world, but smell, taste and color do not separate from its body.

More or less, it is also thus with our white or Red Stone. It does not give any of its own tincture or body to our metals, as it is a heavenly body, just as has been said of the sun. It draws the tincture out of the metals and causes them to reach their extreme power, so that they can turn into seed and produce the Stone thereof. If God had not created full powers in the metals, no change would occur even if you threw the Stone a thousand times on them, because the Stone cannot give what it has not.

I have written that the Stone can be made with many things, and just as the ruby then keeps the name of the ruby, those things will keep their own names. It is nothing but the Stone that is one with crystal-glass. The Stone is only a transposer from bad to good, from the impure to the pure, of everything that is like itself, not in all things but strictly only in metals.

A Right and Perfect Medicine of the Other Order, To Cleanse Copper of All Impurities

Take copper, 20 or 30 lb, beat it into thin lamellae, 5 or 6 times annealed and slaked in urine to make it beautiful and clear, and laminated thinly like pennies. When it is annealed, there must not be left any scales or impurity. It must be clear and red. Thereafter, dry it well with a cloth and then in the sun or near the fire. After this, take good pulverizes white auripigment, powder it finely on the Stone with oil, like black soap. Coat the copper sheets with it and dry them near the fire. Coat and dry them again, and do this 4 or 5 times. Now take common salt, called pore salt, pulverize it, stratify it in a crucible, the crucible completely filled, then lute the crucible. Do the same with the other crucibles, as many as you wish. Put them in a calcination furnace, first with a small fire, then with a stronger, but keep it up till they glow through and through. Let them stand thus in the red-hot heat for 24 hours, then let them cool, take them out, edulcorate the laminae with warm water to make them lose any taste of salt. Now dry them well and pound or rub them finely, like paint.

Keep at hand 2 or 3 big cupels, it must be cups, put the laminae into them and pour clean water on the matter, stir it well, let it sink, pour it off again, to the first water, and continue doing this till the matter is clear. Then dry the powder and mix it with sal alkali, borax, and (|), put it in a sack such as is here illustrated, filling it completely. Sew it together and stick a small wooden spigot into it. Lute the sack all around with good glue, as thick as two fingers' breadth, so that the glue can stand the fire. Let it dry well, set it in a furnace on two irons, put a crucible underneath it at the place where you have stuck the spigot, and stir the fire in the hearth strongly. The matter will easily melt and flow into te crucible. Continue doing this till all your powder has been turned into one body. Thereafter weigh it and add to every ounce one 3j of fine Luna as it comes out of the cupel. Smelt it together in a big crucible, pour it into a strong mold, and your body is ready and alive, and prepared for the medicine of the second order and effect, according to the teachings of Hermes and Geber.

Ad Rubeum

There were some artists who took Roman vitriol, 1 lb, calx of Saturn, and mercury sublimated to the Red, 1 lb, vitriol 1 oz, ad pondus omnius. Prepare of these an AF to the White, as said above, and when the water has been thus made, extract the salt from the Death's head as before, keep the water and the salt each separate till they are needed. Then take 1 lb of mercury, sublimate it through 3 lb of dry vitriol and rub it also so the second time among the faeces on the stone. The third time, take fresh vitriol and sublimate it. Do this three times, and the mercury will have been sublimated 9 times and be well prepared.

Now take 1 lb of calx of Saturn, calcined so much with vinegar or in the sun that it becomes impalpable. Mix it with the salt of the Death's Head and proceed immediately as with the oil to the White, except that this one must stand much longer in the fire than the White. The fire must also be stronger or the fixation of the oil. In other respects the manipulations o the opus are everywhere the same. Test to see if it is fixed, and when it is fixed, you have a great secret. Here no purification or ablution occurs, because the faeces consume themselves, and an oil will remain eternally, somewhat subtler than honey. This oil cannot be turned into a Stone like those made with Aqua Vitae. Here too, many corrosives are contained within, and it should be noted that the Sol made with this oil and transmuted out of imperfect metals cannot be used for any medicine.

Another Oil to the Red from AF and Saturn

There were other artists who took vitriol 3 lb, saltpeter 2 lb, and prepared of it an AF. They pulverized the Death's Head and put it in a glass, added an alembic wit a hole and poured the water back on it, then drew it off again with strong fire and kept it. Then they took 1 lb of lead, and 2 lb of mercury, amalgamated both and dissolved it again, set it in the balneum, drew it off, poured it on again, and continued doing this till the matter turned into a red oil and no longer coagulated.

Then they also took 1 oz of Sol, dissolved it in AR, and poured it on the red oil, shook it between their hands and mixed it well, set it in sand, and again drew the AF off. Then they sealed the glass as well as possible, set it in the tripod, gave it as much fire as is used for keeping lead in flux. They continued doing this till the oil was fixed. This oil, 1 part to 8, tinges into a most perfect oil which can stand all tests.

A Precious Oil to the Red

Dear Sons, you should know the following and consider it a great secret. Take 3 lb of Vitriol Virid. Aer., Plumbum Album an. 5 lb, Croci Pulv. Lapidis Haematite 3j 4. Saltpeter ad pondus omnium. Crush them so that they mingle thoroughly; divide them into three parts. From one of the parts, make an AF; in a glass vessel and no other kind of vessel. After this, pour it on the other part of the matter (a second part) and draw it over on a strong fire. Pour this now onto the third part of the matter and keep this water well closed.

Pulverize the Death's Head and rub them with ammonia * water, which I will each later on, on a marble, till they are quite small, as if one wished to paint with the matter. Let it dry in a room or by the sun; grind it once again and put it into an alembic. Pour your water on it, draw it off again, first with a gentle fire for 24 hours; then gradually with stronger fire, till the matter begins to glow. After this, keep it in a steady glow for 6 weeks. Then let it cool down, remove it and preserve it.

After this, take the Death's Head and the remaining faeces. Powder them and moisten with vinegar and draw off its salt as you know how to do, so that no faces stay behind. When your salt is clear, pour the AF on it, give it gentle heat on sand or on ashes for 12 hours. Follow this with stronger heat for 6 hours, so that it will glow mildly. Then let it cool off. Take the water in the recipient and close it well. Again rub the faeces with vinegar, and afterwards dissolve it in vinegar; put it in the balneum. Do as you have been instructed before and see it if produces faeces. Coagulate it and pour the AF back on it. Draw it off, Repeat 3 or 4 times and the salt together with the water will go over the helm.

Do believe me that I have worked wonder with this water, which cannot be described here. I have personally turned this water into a red crystal which gave off a light at night by which a whole table of people could see enough to eat their meal by. Keep it until you need it, and consider it a treasure of all waters.

More so take Merc. Praeparati of its humidity, for each pound of mercury, 2 pounds of vitrioli Romani and sublime it therewith. Mix it again with the faeces and for the third time, take fresh vitriol and sublime it again. Do this 4 or 5 times, the more times the better. After this, the mercury is ready. Take then, one ounce of sol, thinly beaten and cut into rolls. Dissolve it into the AF which you have made, and set it into a basin with sifted ashes. Put the basin into a kettle filled with very warm water, and in an hour the mercury will dissolve.

Take one ounce of the sublimated mercury, dissolve it also in this water. After this, throw another ounce of your mercury in and let this also dissolve. Then it is enough as you will have 3 ounces of matter dissolved in it, 1 oz of Sol and 2 oz of mercury. Now put a helm on together with a recipient, draw the water off, pour it back on again until it will no longer go over in balneo. Let it cool down and put it on a furnace and ashes. Continue this so long as the water will go over. In this distillation you will see wonders, because you will see all the colors of the whole world in the helm. The colors are in the spirit and the corpus keeps the spirit in it and with it. The colors are covered in the corpus as you will learn in Vegetabili. Search for it in Chapter 93.

When no more drops are coming, let it cool down, remove the helm and close the glass well above. Set it in tripode for 40 days; the heat should be such that you can easily keep you hand in the furnace. Your matter will become fixed within this time, and when it is cold, it will be hard as glass. As soon as it gets near heat that will melt like wax, it flows as if it were wax or as an oil. This is a perfect Lapis Compositus, and no foreign things have been added to it which are not part of its kind or species. My child should not that at least one part of this Stone falls on 1000 parts or more. I myself have worked in his area and have accomplished the operation one time. It is such a beautiful Stone to behold and shines so much at night that one does not have a need for light. This is why it is such an excellent Medicine and a noble Stone and should be considered a great Secretum. The Water Salis Armon., with which the above mentioned powder is to be rubbed or ground, is made in the following way. Take one lb of *; 2 lb of vitriol and sublimate them together. And again mix the matter with the faeces. For the third time, take fresh vitriol and sublimate this also 4 times, Grind this sublimated * to powder, put it into a glass, pour distilled vinegar upon it, just enough vinegar to dissolve it and no more. Now the water is as yellow as Sol when it has been sublimed through Vitriol. The Vitriol acetum destillatum produces the Tincture of Sol. This then is the water which you must rid you Death's head, as indicated above, which is to be imbibed with this * Water. It gives good Ingress.

The Salts of the Metals

Up to now, dear Son, you have heard how you are to proceed with and handle the great Work with Amalgamations and with certain Olea. Now you will hear how to make salts out of the metals that can also produce a perfect Elixir, as good as the Olea, although its projection is not as high. It is an easy work, however, and takes but a short time. After that, I will teach you how to make the Stone, which I consider my greatest Secretum.

Look for further instructions in the Vegetabili. This is the reason why it is necessary to preserve the green of the Vitriol. If you were to coagulate it, part of its greenness would be taken from it; for it would become yellow, wile yet the green is in the Quintesentia that we seek in the Vitriol. That is why you must permit it to dry and sprout in a room. Then its greenness is covered with the white, for as soon as it becomes moist again, its greenness will reappear, This the outermost of the Vitriol must be turned into the innermost, and the innermost must come out, in order to preserve its soul and its spirit and to retain its Quinta Essentia. This is a great Mysterium or Secretum in our Art. When the Vitriol has thus been cleansed, it is as red as a rose or ruby. It has within itself the four elements in the perfection, and this is the stone which God has given us for nothing.

You should now take the white powder which you were told to put aside and place it in a phial and close it with Sigillo hermetis. Set it in ashes and heat it by a lamp, as warm as the sun shines in the midst of summer. Keep it thus, until you see that it begins to turn yellow. Let it stand yet another ten days and see if it dies not begin to tinge a red color. Then, increase the fire a little, and if it becomes more red, let it stand in the regimen of the fire as is. If, however, it does not become somewhat redder in 8-10 days, increase the fire by one lamp until the color increases. If it stays the same, add yet another lamp, thus each time increasing the heat by degrees until the color changes to a rose or ruby red.

When it has become a high or deep red color, let it stand yet another 8-10 days in the same heat and watch if the color does not change into a color different than red. Now the matter has been reversed and its innermost has been brought outside. In this way, you will not lose the greenness if it has been reversed into redness. This is because it is in the deepest inner parts and can no more be brought out. It will forever stay red and unfixed; for if it were fixed, everything would be lost, because it would have to be dissolved in water and coagulated again, and afterwards distilled over the helm.

I am telling you that I have never revealed to you greater secrets than this! I am telling you, by my God, that this Secret has never been set down into writing by the philosophi except by my hand alone. Moreover, I am telling you that there is no greater secret in art than this. Therefore, I beseech you and all those who will understand it, that you will never bring it to light except where it is right to reveal it, by the damnation of your soul, for it is a Secret above all Secrets. Since with this matter all metals can be turned into oil, when they are dissolved in AF, when the calx has been beaten to the bottom and processed as required.

All Olea Metallorum turn red as blood, without Luna and [...] not lead, for all metals are red in their innermost, but one is redder than the other. When they have been brought to redness, you must dissolve them, again coagulate them until they are free from all faeces and they have their elements perfectly joined; for once they have arrived at this stage, nothing is left but faces. The earth, too, has become subtle and liquid and is dissolved in the other three.

When they have thus been made subtle, with dissolving and coagulating, you can distill it over the helm to a red oil, as you will learn. As you are working with Vitriol, you must also treat mercury. After it has been dissolved in AF, beaten down, decanted from its saltiness and dried, you can put it in a glass the same as has been done with the Vitriol. Or you can put a Sublimated Mercury into such a glass, proceed in the same way and cleanse it of its faeces, and distill it over into a red oil. In the same way copper can be processed. What do you think? Is this not a great Secret? Never before has anything like it been heard. Open your ears therefore, listen and understand!

Now we will return to our work. When you see that your matter remains in an Oily state, take it out of the ashes and put it into another, strong glass. Pour a goodly amount of wine vinegar upon it, and set it into the balneum to boil for 4 days, often stirring it with a wooden spoon. After the fourth day, let it cool down and settle. Decant off the clear liquid and pour more vinegar upon the remaining faeces. Add more distilled vinegar, and repeat three times. Now throw away the faeces and put an alembic upon the glass containing the solution; draw off the vinegar, so that the matter becomes quite dry. Now you have the matter at the bottom of the glass and much more beautiful than before. Again, pour fresh vinegar upon it, and treat it as above. Reiterate this until no more faeces remain in the Solution. Then coagulate it to a dry powder, put a helm on it with a large head and distill. First you will obtain a yellow spiritus, then red oils and finally a white spiritus. Let the matter cool down, remove the receiver and its contents. It is the blessed oil. Preserve it well until you need it for your metallic salt.

At the bottom of the alembic you will find a matter that is as white as snow and is clear as crystal. It is the rectified matter of the aforesaid material. It can be pulverized and imbibed into the red oil as into its own corpus. Put it in vitreum apullam and hang it in tripodem for 40 days in moderate heat. Now it will coagulate into a Lapis Philosophorum which will dissolve all metals into Sol. But we will not do this now, but will work toward our Salt and Oil of metals in this manner, as with Vitriol. Thus the element of earth will go over with the oil, red as blood. This the earth of Vitriol does not do, as its oil separates from the earth. Consequently God has given it such benediction that from it alone can one make the Lapis Philosophorum without any Addition. But first one has to fix the oil with its earth. That does not happen in metals, because their earth goes over the helm together with the fire, and the whole body reverses, which tinges the metals into perfect Sol.

By the same process, you can make the Oil of Mercury and Copper, and the earth also goes over the helm in the oil and stays in the oil for all eternity. With this oil, you can perform such miracles as would be too lengthy to recount here. You well know what is said about the oil Veneris. Yet the oil from mercury is much better in its effects than the oil Veneris.

Now We will Return to Our Work of the Salts and Prepare Them into Oil with the Help of Oil of Vitriol and Their Mercury Sublimated from Them.

Take the Mercury and dissolve it in AF, made of equal parts of vitriol and salt peter. Then put it in a glass retort, add a big alembic, put it in sifted ashes, and make a small fire underneath. Distill the AF off, and increase the fire to let the Mercury distill. Let it cool and take the Mercury out. Put it in a long-necked glass, just as you do with Vitriol. Put it in a long-necked glass, just as you do with Vitriol. Set it in ashes, make a lamp-fire underneath, and let it stand thus till it is perfectly red. Dissolve and coagulate it, as has been taught regarding the vitriol. When it is clean, distill it to a red oil, not leaving any faeces behind. All metals are processed in the same way as has been taught about Mercury.

When the oil of mercury has been drawn over, put your salt and elixir of (-) in a big retort over a gentle heat, to allow the salt to melt. This will happen easily as soon as the heat is such the wax would melt. When it is melted, pour the oil of mercury into it by drops, and they will immediately conjoin as they are pure and clean.

Now you have conjoined Soul and Body in One. They will never again separate, because here the Body receives its own Spirit and fixes it in one moment. Let the glass stand thus on the furnace for 16 to 26 days, in gentle heat, just as if you were to keep wax in flux, without foam. Within this time the substance will be converted into oil which looks like thick honey or like dark red blood, and it will remain thus forever. Now rejoice, my children, you have the secret of all secrets. It does projection in Sol at the rate of 1 part to 1000.

If you intend to make a projection, you must know that you must do it on a body and not on mercury, because the oil would not turn Mercury into a Body for reasons that are not explained here, as they are sufficiently indicated in the treatise on projection. You must take a red-hot copper or silver, or antimony sheet, dribble the oil upon it, and put it on hot coal. The oil will permeate it like water a sponge, and it will be changed into Sol, which can stand all tests.

It does not effect any projection on tin and lead, because the medicine must first disembody the bodies, changing them into its own natures, before it can change them into a Corpus. We will not speak about this here, as it is sufficiently explained elsewhere. What do you think of this secret? Never has anything like it been found in the world.

You have heard how and why you must dissolve the metals and beat them down again into calx, and how you must edulcorate the calx of the AF and sublimate its Mercury, and dissolve the salt in vinegar, then rectify it of its faeces, and how it must afterwards be calcined in a sealed glass to its perfect redness, then dissolved in vinegar, the faeces discarded which it has in it inmost redness and which at first did not let go of it till its innermost had been brought to the outside.

For you must know that everything contains two kinds of faeces. First, in its crudeness, when it was still raw, as when you first dissolved and coagulated vitriol, it was still green and without faeces, but now that it turns red and is again dissolved, it leaves faeces which had not been noticed before. Now someone might ask: How is it that the innermost does not let for of its faeces, although the whole material is clear water? Understand this as follows: When the material is dissolved, it is all outside, and it locks the heat within so that it cannot let go of it. But when the heat is brought out and then dissolved, it opens of its own and lets go of its faces ~ while they are not overcome by the cold. Therefore, you must rectify twice if you wish to prepare a proper Elixir or Quinta Essentia, no matter with what material you are working, spirits, rocks, roots, sugar, honey, etc. And I swear to you by God that such a Secret has never been revealed, nor has anything been written about it except by myself alone, by my hand.

Furthermore, you have also heard how vitriol has to be set to distill, and that oil, red as blood, will go over and the earth be left behind, which is thereafter to be imbibed into its oil and set in the tripod.

In addition, I instructed you to preserve the oil carefully. Moreover, I told you to dissolve Mercury in AF, beat it down, edulcorate it, dry it, put it in vitriol, again imbibe its Corpus with it to turn it all into oil and cause it to achieve projection. I have told you that all metals can be worked in this way and turned into oil without separating the elements. Dear Sons, consider all the words that I have written about this Work, because you stand greatly in need of understanding this well.

I have taught you how you should draw all metals per alembicum, so that they go over without any Death's Head. This is achieved by the strong spirit of vinegar, completely rectified and separated from all its faces inside and outside. When the metals have thus been opened and made subtle, and their innermost is outside, their Elements cannot be separated, and even if you tried everything in the world, you could not part them because of their subtlety and purity. For when they have with them the subtle spirit of vinegar, they go with it through the alembic. If, however, you put them near the fire when there is no spirit of vinegar with them, they congeal together. But while the vinegar is in their pure and subtle Corpus, they turn into oil and congeal the spirit of vinegar with them. Know that the spirit of vinegar is the subtlest spirit in the world, 1000 times subtler than the spirit of brandy. It cannot be kept in any vessel, but if it is already half-fixed, it congeals easily together with the materia to which it is added, as is proven in the Vegetable Work, where wine and its nature are being discussed. There you are also taught what the spirit of the distilled vinegar is, and how it dissolves all things.

Now We Shall Tell You, Dear Children How to Multiply the Philosophical Oil

Take the Philosophical Oil, put it in a big retort. On 1 part pour 100 parts of oil of vitriol, lute and close it tightly above, set it in ashes, and light a fire underneath it, as hot as if you were to keep wax melting, without foaming. Keep it thus continually for 6 weeks, and it will congeal during this time. It will make as good and high a projection as the first did.

Read this over often and bear it in mind, as you will need it for other things, for in this lies hidden the foundation of all arts. But if you wish to draw a good oil out of the metals, as is taught in connection with vitriol, you must dissolve your metal in AF, beat it down, dry and coagulate it, put it in a phial, set it in ashes, and proceed with the regulation of the fire as is taught of vitriol, till it is quite red. Now dissolve it in distilled vinegar and coagulate it till no more faeces are left. Then set it to distill, and the metal will completely turn into oil. It is a perfect Philosophical Oil, though its projection is not as high as that of the first oil prepared from salt. You must multiply all metal oils with oil of vitriol, as it is taught, and in this way you can make much oil, and its projection is quite high. Thank God and do not misuse His gifts, for the sake of your soul's salvation.

Purification and Separation of the Metals from Their Faeces

Know that there are three ways of separating a thing from its faeces. The first way is the way of Nature herself, for nature discards everything that is imperfect, as may be seen every day, when everything buried in the earth it turned into earth — which her means. Look at all the roofs that are standing in the air, be they made of iron, steel, lead, wood, or stone, or anything else, exposed to the air day and night — it deteriorates and turns into nothing with the passage of time, be it fortresses or castles. No matte how strong you are, they are all calcined into earth as their middle degree. But someone might ask: Why not also into air, water, or fire? Know that everything that is here below the circle of Luna is composed of the four Elements, and all the four Elements are impure and full of faeces. Also, one Element is impurer than another, as is reported in the Vegetable Work. Among them, Earth is the impurest and driest Element, containing the most faeces. That is why all things must first be converted into earth before turning them into Air, Water, or Fire. It has to be so, because Nature does not act except from degree to degree. No one can move from the beginning to the end before suffering the middle which lies between them. You can therefore not reach the fourth degree before passing the second and the third. Whoever does not understand this, is advised not to work in our Art. Thus all things that are purified according to the course of Nature first change into Earth. When a thing is transformed into Earth, it is open, and each Element can be extracted, as is proven in the Vegetable Work. If a thing is to be transformed from the first degree into the second, it is necessary to transform it into another nature — unless it has first become Earth. This is so on account of the faeces contained in it.

Take the example of lead. When you stir it on the fire, it must first turn into Earth or ashes before becoming glass. For lead cannot become glass, it must first be earth. This is due to the faeces contained in it. You can make Luna of lead, but it must first become glass, as is taught in many places. Saturn can also be turned into Luna in other ways of its faeces are removed, as is sufficiently taught elsewhere, for lead is Luna in its innermost, and nothing is required except that its faeces separated from it, also its sulphur, which is earthy. Then it is good Luna like that which Nature transforms every day, as may be seen.

Look at the old chapels formerly covered with lead ～ which may have covered them for 600 years. It has been transformed into earth and laid white on the lead. One can see it every day on the old lead roofs. It jumps off in the form of small slates, and if it were to stay there still longer, Nature would finally cook and purify it. I myself have seen that when such an old roof covered with lead ～ and about 2000 years old ～ was dismantled, it was as white as if it had been calcined, and when it was broken into pieces, it looked like filed silver. When it was put on the cupel with other lead, everything together was good silver. Thus Nature had purified it by long digestion, and consumed and destroyed all its faeces, like the dust of the sun.

As an example use a big jar measuring 10 or 12 quarts. Fill it with water, and when the sun is shining, put it in the air day and night. Close it tightly to prevent any air or rain from entering it. The water will become evil-smelling, impure, slimy, and of a bitter taste. In time the taste will consume and destroy itself. The faeces or earthly material in the water will be separated from the watery substance and sink to the bottom. The water will become beautiful and clear as if it were distilled, and it will again be sweet and fragrant Then pour it off into a fine glass, let it stand thus for some time, and it will produce more faeces. Pour it off again, and continue doing this till no more faeces are found at the bottom. Now the water is rectified. And if it were to stand till Doomsday, it would no longer be corrupted.

The same applies to the oils. If they were left standing for several years, they would become clear of all faeces, just as has been said of the water.

See also how old wine or old beer being well preserved and stoppered discards its faeces and yeast. Take some old wine purified of its mother ~ how vigorous and strong it is. And if it were left tightly closed for several years, it would purify itself, so that one would finally find neither faeces nor yeast in it. In time it would become like crystal and red as a ruby and without any faeces. Further details in the Vegetable Work.

Secondly. There is still another way of purifying everything that contains faeces. It is done by the Art. Consequently, the Art comes to the Aid of nature. It is done by dissolving and coagulating, as is partly explained in the Great Work. I will therefore not write more about the separation and purification of the faeces. You will find further information in the Vegetable Work at the place where the rectification of metals is dealt with.

Thirdly. My Child must know that there exists still another rectification for separating the faeces from all metals and minerals. It is done by fire. We will only say as much about this rectification as is necessary. You will also find clearer instructions in the vegetable Work, in connection with the manufacture of precious stones and gems.

Therefore, know that all metals can be cleansed of their faeces by fire, when the elements stay completely together without being separated. Afterwards they can be fixed, and all this is done by fire. It can be done in many ways. Sol must be calcined differently fro Luna; and Luna must be worked differently from lead, and copper differently from antimony. My Child must know that two kinds of calcinations can be done with metals, one by cementing ⁓ which will be discussed later in its treatise ⁓ and one with salt and mineral spirits, without converting the metals into glass, and yet one is different from the other.

All metals are turned into glass without any additive, except only Sol, which does not turn into glass even if it were burnt to Doomsday. Something has to be added which the others do not require, because Sol is pure by nature. Yet it contains a few faeces, though not so many that they would cover the Corpus. No matter how strongly it is burnt, the faeces will not turn into glass. It would rather burn up completely and turn into nothing before becoming glass. That, however, is not the case with the other metals which would of course become glass. Now someone might ask: If a thing has become glass, has it reached its extreme state? Because when a thing has turned into glass, it cannot be converted into any other materia, because glass is the extreme form of all things. At Doomsday, everything below the sky will be converted into glass, as God has ordained. Therefore it is clear that glass is the ultimate matter of all things and cannot be turned into anything else by the Art, except a burnt-out material or faces.

I have often seen that glass was turned into black slag, like iron slag, by long and strong burning; and by still longer burning it became white ash, light as dust, so that it flew away and the glass came to nothing. This it would appear that glass is the ultimate matter of all things, metallic things not excepted. It is the primary substance of all combustible things. Therefore the mild and natural moisture separate from the earth by strong burning, while from metals and minerals the oil does not separate from the earth in the fire but always stays together with it. If the oil would leave the earth and the metallic salts were fusible, how then could they give ingress and tinctures?

Know then that if salt is extracted from the metals and is prepared as it should, there may well result no tincture, but it does projection to the White. The reason is: The oil is locked in the salt like the yellow in the egg. If you wish to make a red tincture, the fire or the oil must be brought outside, and its salt or earth brought inside. Then it will make projection to the Red, just as it had previously made to the White. Before, 1 part fell on 100, now it is 1 part to 1000. And yet it is only one and the same material, only its innermost has been brought outside.

But someone might ask: If the salt or oil is extracted from the metals by means of the fire, its mercury or air I separated from the earth and the oil ~ how then can the salt of oil ive ingress, when the Philosophers say that the air gives ingress, the fire the tincture, the oil melts, the earth congeals ~ yet here the air has flown away due to the long heat of the fire?

Know that enough air has remained with the oil I the fire, that is, as much as is necessary, because the Elements are so well conjoined that you can never separate them. They stay mixed together ~ no fire is found without air, nor air without fire. In addition, earth and fire are two fixed elements; that is why they retain as much air as they require to make ingress.

How then is it, someone might say, that all metals turn into glass, except Sol? The reason is that all metals are impure and full of faeces. That is why they are calcined, as all metallic parts are full of sulfurous faeces which easily overcome them in the ores. When they are put in a mighty fire, they are easily calcinced, and the moisture of the fat sulphurous faeces burns up. The faeces became so dry that the whole metal converts into earth and calx, and if they did not change into calx, they could never become glass, because they have to be calx first.

Nothing can be changed into another nature except by some means. While it had been metal before, now it is glass ~ indeed two natures. If it is to be done, it must be done by a means, which is the earth or the calx of the metal. By strong and long calcinations it is converted into glass, as is taught in the counterfeiting o stones. And when the stones are counterfeited, they look ten times more beautiful and clearer than oriental ones.

For look at the Amusen which are mixed with them, how beautiful green, blue, yellow, red, and white they are, and one is more beautiful and precious than the other. They still consists of metal only. How then is it that one is more beautiful and precious than another, also more fusible? In this connection you must know: When the metal is calcined and is then put in the vaulted furnace or the reverberatory, it requires strong heat before it changes into beautifully clear and transparent glass and before the faeces are cleared. The more it is cleared, the more beautiful and fusible it becomes. And you must know that the glass made in this way is like a glorious Corpus, while before it had been a black impure Corpus, and under this Corpus lies hidden the noble Quinta Essentia of the metal. The latter is incombustible, shining with its lovely color till Judgment Day. Its soul, therefore, is in a glorified Corpus, just like a light in a crystal lantern, and one soul shines much brighter than another.

Therefore you must know that the Quinta Essentia or the incombustible oil of the metal together with its clear salt shine out of the metallic glass like a candle out of a lantern, and the more beautiful it is, the more easily it flows. Furthermore, you must understand that when the metal is calcined and the master wishes to prepare a green Amausen from it, it must be made with Venus. And if he wishes to have a beautiful green in color and clarity over everything green, he must rub the calx on a marble slab with salt water till it is impalpable. Thereafter it is washed again till no earthly rot comes off. Now burn some glass from it, and it will be a beautiful Amausen which will melt more easily than if you had rubbed and washed it. The same is to be done with the other kinds of calx, such as that of lead and copper. They result in a yellow glass, tin in white glass, silver blue, gold red, and if you wish to obtain other kinds of calx, mix them with another color.

Now someone might ask: When the metals have thus turned into glass, and while glass is the ultimate matter of things, can it again be changed into a Corpus? Know then that it can easily be turned back into a Corpus, because there had been little calcinations. Every metal can easily be turned into glass or Amausen within 12 hours in a reverbaration furnace, because the metallic calx is not yet opened. When the earth has been extracted, the material is dry. The more rotten and impure the metal is, such as copper, the dryer the calx is. When it makes contact with the heat of the flames, there s nothing or very little of a metallic nature that can escape. And while the Corpus is not yet opened, the strong fire forces it to turn into glass. Thus the mercury of the metals cannot escape anywhere. Before it can rise out of the dry calx, the faeces have already become glass.

That is why in many works where it has to be reverberated, it is calcined by not giving it stronger heat than to make it glow, because if the fire were stronger, it would turn into glass. Note further: Take the Amausen and powder them finely. Take some good distilled vinegar in which ammoniac is dissolved ~ in 1 lb of vinegar 1 Lot of *. Rub the glass with it on a stone as you do with paint. Thereafter put it in a glass or stone jar, pour on it a good amount of distilled vinegar, set it in the Balneum, and let it boil, stirring frequently. Let it stand thus a day and night, and let it cool, pour the vinegar off the faeces into a clean jar. Again pour fresh vinegar on these faces, and do this three times. Now the vinegar off by the alembic, and the Corpus of the metals is left at the bottom of the glass in the form of a powder. Mix it with borax, put it in a crucible, and melt it with a strong fire into a Corpus. If it is iron or copper, it is beautiful and pure, does not leave any slag, nor does it rust, and it is rid of all faeces. If it is tin, its imperfection has been removed from it, and it is pure and strong like silver. If it is silver, it is fixed; if gold, it is a medicine; if lead, it is silver, etc.

But in so doing, nothing useful has been produced, except that Nature is being researched. I have seen that 1 3j of the red Amausen has been given for 20 Ducats; 3jj of the blue for 20 Ducats; of the green for 8 ducats, and of the others 1 3j for 2 ducats.

It is therefore not necessary to turn it back into a Corpus. It is part of the subtle art of making Amausen and it goes fast,

120

requiring little time if they are made of the red calx of copper, lead, tin, and iron, and they can be sold for 1 Ducat a lb. But if the calx is purified as taught in the Vegetable Work, precious stones can be made of it, which can be turned into drinking cups for Princes and vessels for Kings and Lords. Consequently, the metals are purified by calcining and reverbarating, the calx is washed, then is turned back into a Corpus, again calcined and washed till no more faeces comes off.

Commentary

Know further that there is still another way of calcining. It is called cementation, which is a calcinations. But there is a difference, because in the common calcinations you take prepared salt of gem and metal laminae, and stratify both till the crucible is full. Then the crucible is well luted and set n the fire in natural heat. If it is copper, 2 days; if it silver, 24 hours; if it is tin, 8 days; if it is lead, 2 days, etc. This is the way to calcine.

The *modus caementatis*, the way to cement, however, is like the above, but the difference is that it is aided by mineral spirits which help the fire burn the metals and reduce them to calx. It is also done in order to give the Body a tincture to make it melt more easily. Mix the spirits with the prepared salt, then proceed in the previous manner. I have indicated this so that you may well understand the regimen of the metals in the fire. There are still many more ways for bringing the metals to perfection by the fire, which it is not necessary to know for our present work. You may read about them in the Vegetable Book, Chap 6.

The Philosophers' Stone

Now I will teach you a work which I have done with my own hands, and it is an easy Work to carry out, without much effort and worry. It is one of my secrets, and whoever cannot prepare this Work, will never accomplish anything in the Art. For here I teach what the Philosophers call Mercury, and how it is to be extracted from the Corpus, also other secrets which will be disclosed in the Work, and how to separate and congeal the faeces of Sol and Luna by fire, then amalgamate them with Mercury, and change them in a short time into the Philosophers' Stone. First I will teach you how to prepare Sol and Luna to give Mercury a Body, ten how to conjoin tem in the Work.

The Fixation of Luna

First, you must take fine Luna from the cupel and fine Sol at your discretion. Beat them into thin laminae as thick as an Orint and half a hand wide. To Luna add prepared sal gemmae and auripigment for the White, sublimated with + and an equal amount of Lapis Calaminaris. Through 3 lb of that sublimate 1 lb of auripigment is ready. Now take 3j of the auripigment to 1 lb of prepared salt and 3ij of white calcined tartar, which must be quite clear and transparent. Mix everything well together with this powder, put layer upon layer in a good crucible with silver laminae, as you know, the thickness of a finger. Lute it well and set it to calcine in moderate heat, so that the silver does not melt. Let it stand thus for 36 hours, then let it cool, and break the crucible open. The Luna is black and brittle like glass. Now take clean water and wash the blackness and saltiness off from the silver, let it dry, and pound it in a mortar. Then rub it well with distilled water, take a glass bowl and put the pulverized silver into it. Wash it well with clean water and let it sit for some time or pour it off into another glass. Pour fresh water on the powder, sir it and wash it off into another glass. Pour fresh water on the powder, stir it and wash it till the water runs off as clear as it was when you poured it on. Now the silver is washed and is as white as snow. If you believe that some of it has gone back into the water, dry and melt it again, and you will get the remaining silver back.

Now take the white-washed silver, reduce it with borax, laminate it again and cement it pulverized, wash and melt it again as before, and continue doing this till the silver stays white in the cement and no rottenness or blackness comes off it when it is washed. In this way the silver gets rid of all its faces without being separated. Try this in the following way: Dissolve 3j of this silver in rectified wine or Quinta Essentia, coagulate and dissolve it again, and you will not find any faeces, even if you repeated it a hundred times.

What do you think of this secret? It is a great secret in the Art. I am telling you truly, it is the greatest secret of all in the Art, more so than one can understand. The Elements are rectified without separation, and you can make an Elixir from one metal only, because it has its own proportion of weights. When the Elements are purified with solving and coagulating, it is very good, but my method is much surer, because in working with dissolving and coagulating, the element is separated together with the faeces and the three other Elements. If is a good thing if its done correctly and carefully, and if care is taken to preserve everything, to lose nothing, and that the fire is well regulated during reverberation in order to rectify the earth, so that fire, water, air can be extracted therefrom. It requires careful attention to prevent anything from being lost. When it does happen, however, you no longer have the right weight of the Elements and you will never reach a happy end. Keep this well in your hearts so that you may never forget it, for there must not be any weakness, the Elements must have the oil their own weight and proportion. It is therefore necessary to proceed very carefully in this Work where the Elements have to be separated.

It is indeed good if it is done in this way, and it makes an infinite projection, much higher than when the elements are not separated. Therefore, my Child, many of us have made mistakes and spent much time in vain before they discovered the rectification of the Elements while they are together. That is what I have revealed to you here. Therefore do not take any risks, because I worry that you might go wrong and lose something of the Elements. Then all cost and effort would be lost, as you would find in the end.

Therefore, dear Sons, keep to my method and you cannot go wrong. You may well lose dome of your powder in the washing, but what is left is perfect, because Nature does not miss. The Elements remain united and are even ore closely bound together by the Work than they were before. For when they are pure and rid of their faeces and they are set to cement 3 times, they will be so well congealed together than Luna will be fixed.

Test it in AF ～ it does not attack Luna ～ It retains its colors and also passes through copper. Calcination and cementation can also be made with prepared common slat, without arsenic or tartar, but it takes longer. And if you do it only with salt without arsenic and tartar, Luna will not readily cement and calcine. It has to be repeated several times ～ about 3 times ～ before Luna is calcined enough to be rubbed. That is why arsenic and tartar are added, as they are sharp and work easily through the laminae, so that the cementation must not be repeated often. Thirdly, they result in a white tincture suitable for a White Work. But if a Red Work is intended, I would be better to take Mercury to the Red than arsenic, just as is done in the sublimation of Sol. This then is the reason why arsenic is added to the salt; though, if ever you wished, you could achieve it with salt alone. I myself have frequently tested and done it. There is no difference in the cementation of Luna and Sol, except that mercury to the Red is used instead of auripigment. Also, Sol must not be pulverized and washed like Luna, and Sol does not contain any blackness because tartar, mercury and the salt consumes all its faeces. Then you Sol is rid of all its faeces, just like Luna. Thus you have all your cement perfect and together and well purified. Although the separation of the Elements causes a much higher and subtler projection, there is danger involved in it. This purification, however, is sure and without worry.

Now we will return to our Work, and I will first teach you how the Philosophical Mercury is to be extracted. At the beginning I showed you many a Work which other masters have performed, whom I saw working in the laboratory. Some of them are perfect, others imperfect. Be that as it may, it is necessary to have the Philosophical mercury if a good result is to be obtained. For the Mercury which comes from the mines is a crude sperma, not yet sufficiently cooked, and it would have to lie in the earth for another 300 years before it would coagulate; then again, for many more years till it would turn into a powder. Then, by long cooking in natural heat, it would become a vapor. When it is finally a vapor, it passes into the opening of the minerals. When it finds the Philosophical Sulfur with its spiritual nature, it turns into a Corpus. After the Sulfur has been separated from its fattiness, it results in a perfect metal, white or red. The Sulfur of the ignorant is foam and faeces and the combustible fattiness of Vitriol. The latter is separated well by the power of Nature which desire to rid herself of her faeces, to rid the red Sulphur of the foam of the red vitriol, and the white of the white vitriol, as is clearly indicted in the Vegetable Work.

When now the aforesaid mercurial vapor is conjoined with the Philosophical Sulphur, it must still digest and cook for a long time in the bowels of he earth before this Mercury and Sulfur congeal, and this may well take over a thousand years. From this you can now understand that the mineral sulfur is still but a crude thing, from which the seed of the metals is cooked with the help of Nature, before it canes into a spirit. That is why no metal is found in Mercury mines and no

Mercury in metal mines. For Mercury is a raw material, of no use in our Art. It is only an instrument and a hammer to work with in our Art, and a means for extracting the colors from metals and metallic things. But as far as its use in the Art is concerned it is considered raw material and good for nothing for reasons indicated above. I have told you all this so that you should know that all those are wrong who work with such a Mercury.

Extraction of Mercury from Luna

If you wish to extract Mercury from a body, make first an AF with vitriol and Sulfur. In it dissolve Luna, as is customary beat it down with common water, and wash the saltiness off from the calx with clean water, dry it, and put it in a wide-bottomed glass, set it in the Athanor or furnace wherein the spirits are calcined, give it moderate heat such as is used to keep lead melting, and let it stand in such heat for 6 weeks, The Luna will open and mercury will be able to separate from the earth.

You can likewise proceed with Sol, except that Sol must stand for 18 weeks or longer before its Mercury can be separated from its earth and oil, which are always together. For Sol is a solid compact corpus. That s why it must stand longer till it opens. It would therefore be better to let it stand for 30 or 40 weeks. Then it will finally look like a sponge and become as light that it is unbelievable. And if you put calx of Sol in a glass bowl, the glass will be so full that it almost runs over. Then it can be opened and the Mercury can easily be sublimated. In this manner you can open all metals, so that you can extract their Mercury from them by sublimation, as you have heard about the metallic salts.

Clarification of Luna

Sublimate it 3 or 4 times through vitriol or arsenic, and it will become as clear as crystal, of which we will not say any more here. When now Sol and Luna have thus been opened in the calcination furnace, or the athanor, or the tripod, pound them small with *. To 1 lb of calx take 8 Lots of *, which must be clear and transparent, without any moisture. Then put it in a glass. Thereafter take distilled vinegar ~ 5 times distilled ~ containing no faeces. Put it in another glass in which is the calx of Luna, lute the tubes carefully, and let the lute dry. Hen light a fire underneath and slowly distill the vinegar over the calx, always taking 1 ob of Luna to 4 lb of distilled vinegar. When the vinegar has all one over, let it stand cold for 3 days; if you open it sooner, the distilled vinegar and the * will fly away together with Luna, and you will not keep anything. That is how strong the material is, because cold and hot come together.

When you wish to proceed further, put first some cut glass on its mouth that closes tightly, lute it on immediately to prevent the powers from escaping. Then set it in the Balneum and do not give it more fire than will allow you to keep your hand in, and to drink the water without getting burnt. Let it stand thus for 6 weeks, then let it cool, break it open, lute it immediately with an alembic on top and well closed receptacles, and distill it over in the Balneum in moderate heat as ong as something goes over.

Then take it out, set it in ashes, add the receptacle, give it first a small fire, then a stronger one, till Mercury is ready to sublimate together with the * as white as snow. Let it stand thus for 24 hours to allow the Mercury to emerge from the earth. Then let it cool, remove the alembic, and weigh the mass, Thus you will know how much Mercury you have sublimated with the *. Put the sublimate back into a glass and sublimate it again. If any faeces remin, you must sublimate it till nothing is left behind. Preserve this mercury well till you need it.

But in the vessel in which you hve sublimated the Mercury, the earth and the oil of the Corpus are left. Take them out and weigh them, and you will also know how much Mercury you have sublimated from them. Put this earth in a glass and pour enough distilled vinegar over it to dissolve it clearly. If there are any faeces, pour it off, and coagulate and dissolve till there are no more faeces. Then you have a salt a clear as crystal.

Now take the Mercury sublimated with *, and the salt. Rub them together on the marble, thus dry. Then put the substance in a glass bowl and set in the tripod or in the calcinations furnace. Let it stand there for 6 weeks and give it as much heat as if you were to keep lead in flux. At the end of the sixth week, let it cool, put it in a humid cellar, cover it with a linen cloth to prevent any dust from falling into it, and within 6 or 8 days everything will dissolve into clear water. It is the Philosophical Vinegar. My Child must know that this is the right Philosophical Vinegar, and when they write Our Acetum Distillatum, they mean this water, and it is thus of which they write in such a strange way, about which we will not speak here.

Pour this water into a glass, and take 3 parts of Luna prepared in the fire, and 1 part of Sol, prepared as taught. Dissolve each in AF and beat it down, wash and dry it, and dissolve enough of each. For you must know how much you will need. When you have prepared these two kinds of calx, set the glass with the water, or the distilled Philosophical

Vinegar in ashes, and light a small fire underneath, such as is used to dissolve Luna or Sol.

Mixing

Take 3 parts of calx of Luna and 1 part of calx of Sol, mix them together, and put 1 3j or 2 of that in your water. Then if you have such water, and if you wish to achieve a great Work, stopper the glass carefully and dissolve it. When it is almost dissolved, add some more of it till it is no longer dissolved and stays at the bottom. Then it is enough, and your water is saturated with its own food and has drunk its own milk.

You must know that this is the first solution in the world ever to have been discovered, because here no mistake can be made in the proportion of the weights, for as Mercury is dissolved, it at once dissolves all metals, as has been taught in many other places. And it does not dissolve more than it can handle. This is the best amalgamation one can find.

When now the dissolution has been made, take another glass, such as is here illustrated. Into that pour the dissolved material from the remaining powder that is not dissolved and set it as deep in ashes as the matter is in the glass ~ not deeper. Give it heat like that of the sun at noon, and not warmer. Cover the glass with a double linen cloth, and the material will coagulate into a grey powder or mass. When it is coagulated, take a round piece of glass, cut exactly to the mouth of the vessel, lute it with a strong lute, and let it stand thus till you see that your material is turning white. Then increase the fire like the sun in June, and keep it thus in this heat till it as white as snow. Now increase the fire again like the sun in Leo, and wit this heat crystalline longish stones will grow out of your material, like glass or needles. Keep the glass in this heat till you notice that no more crystals grow out of it. Now the material is fixed. You must know that if the crystals do not appear, the material has become fixed with the second heat. Be not concerned about it, for it is better for everything to become fixed in low than in strong heat. For when you first heat like the sun shining in the midst of summer, crystals will shoot as long as a hand and as broad. But that is not good.

It is better to cook the Stone in low heat, so that no crystal points or stones grow out of it. If there grow too many and you give it a little too much heat, the spirit rises in the form of a white vapor and attaches itself above to the glass. When that happens, you must open the glass and scrape the material down again. Take guard not to give it too much heat, so that your material does not rise and turn yellow and red like a pebble. Then it would be spoiled and you would have to start all over. Therefore, see to it that you do not make your fire too strong, so as not to get the yellowness or redness before the whiteness. It is better for the fire to be too small than too big.

When it is now perfectly white and no crystal points shoot out of it, the material is fixed. Divide it into 2 parts, one half to the White, the other to the red. Take the half which you wish to bring to the Red, set it in ashes and bring it to the Red. Pour Paradise Water over the other half to the white, and heat it till the White Stone is perfect ~ before you give the Red its fire. But this you must understand, this Paradise Water must be extracted from Luna, and 9 parts of it must be drawn over 1 part of the White, and cooked therein till it is perfect.

Extraction of Live Mercury from Bodies

Now I will teach you how to make Paradise Water from Luna, and you must know that t is extracted in two ways. The first form of the Work has already been explained, but this one is made in a different way, because this Mercury must go over alive. It is almost done in exactly the same manner, except that instead of * you take clear transparent calcined *, the same weight as *. When you have rubbed the calx Luna with *, you must not put the material for a long time in the calcinations furnace to open it, but you must put it in a glass, pour the vinegar over it, then distill it off, as has been taught before. The mercury will go over in the alembic in drops, because of the power of Nature contained in the *. Put this Mercury into a glass retort and distill its phlegma off, as has been taught before.

Inceration

Thereafter, take it out and pour on 1 part of the white Stone 9 part of Mercury, close it well, set it back in ashes to the other glass which contains the Red Stone, and give it a somewhat stronger fire than the heat of the sun in the summer ~ as if you wished to make rosewater. Do this till your Stone is well boiled and cooked in is own juice and sweat. Then it will no more thirst in all eternity, that is, if the Stone has absorbed the paradise Water and has turned into a powder. Now increase your fire somewhat till the Stone begins to become white. For when the Stone has drunk its milk, its color is between grey and black. Then the fire must be increased by degrees, till the Stone is again perfectly white. This whiteness surpasses the whiteness of snow and looks more like a heavenly color than an artificially produced one. When you see this whiteness, rejoice and thank od for his gifts which He has put in Nature.

After this, remove one half from the glass. Piut the other in a crucible, melt it. It flows as easily as wax. When it is melted, pour it into a wooden mold, coated with sheep's fat or oil, and you have a Stone as clear, hard, and transparent as crystal.

Multiplication of the White

Regarding the half which you left in the glass, multiply it as follows: Take it out and weigh it. To 1 part take 100 parts of Luna prepared in the fire and dissolved in AF, well washed and dried, rubbed on a stone with the medicine. When dry, put it back in a glass, and on 1 part of this material pour 9 parts of Paradise Water extracted from Luna. Again seal the glass, regulate the fire as before when you poured on the first Paradise Water, and continue with the fire till the Paradise Water has been absorbed. Now you can again take half of it out and use it to advantage, again multiplying the other half, one to the Red, the second to the White. But both cannot stand together on a furnace, as the Red requires a stronger heat than the White. The multiplication, however, is the same, except that for the Red the Paradise Water must be extracted from Sol, and for the White from Luna. Thus you can at all times multiply the White and the Red, and tinge with it ~ but use it to the honor of God and the help of the poor.

Purification of the Stone

You know that I told you above to keep half of the Stone for the Red, to pour Paradise Water over the other half, and to set it again in the furnace to the White Stone till the White is accomplished. During this time it turns yellow due to the small fire with which the White Stone is prepared, it cannot become red. Therefore, continue with the fire by degrees till the Stone takes on other colors and becomes somewhat darker due to the yellowness. Keep on increasing the fire till the material is perfectly red, like a ruby, and shines in the glass like fish eyes. And when the signs appear, the Stone is made and fixed. I am telling you this so that you should use the right measure of fire, for if you use too strong a fire, causing the redness to appear before the yellowness, you must begin anew. And if you get the whiteness before the blackness, it is the same.

That is why a small fire is always better than too strong a fire. And proceed only by degrees. As the colors change and heighten the fire is to be increased, and this not only applies to our Work but to all others as well. The right regulation of the fire is the second masterpiece of our Art, and unless the proportion is carefully observed, everything is lost.

When the material is fixed and as red as a ruby, take it out and increate it with fire paradise Water extracted from Sol, just as has been said about Luna. Pour 9 parts of Paradise Water over 1 part of the Red Stone, seal the glass above with strong lute, set it back in the furnace in the ashes, and give fire as if you were to keep lead melting, till it has absorbed all the Paradise water. Now it has turned into a grey powder – – rather black than grey. Keep the fire at the same heat till the powder is quite white. Now increase your fire considerably till you see the matter turn yellow. Then increase the fire by degrees somewhat more, till the powder is dark yellow. When al your powder is brown like saffron, so that it cannot get any yellower, increase your fire considerably till you see the red color appear. Continue with the fire till it is perfectly red like a ruby. Now rejoice, because the Stone to the Red is made. Let it cool.

Take one half out and leave the other half to multiply. Put what you have taken out in a crucible, let it melt, and pour it into a small glass coated with grease, pour the Stone into it, and it will be as hard as glass and as red as a ruby. Take 1 part of it, throw it in 2000 parts of lead, and it will turn into the best Sol, as highly colored as has ever been seen, and it can stand all tests and examination. Thank God.

Multiplication to the Red

Thereafter, set the other half to multiply. To 1 part of the Stone take 200 parts of your calcined or cemented Sol, dissolve, wash, and dry it, then melt it under the Stone, put it back into the glass, and pour on it some of the solar Paradise Water ~ 9 times as much as there is of the mixed materia. Lute your glass carefully and give it fire just as if you were to keep lead melting, as has been taught before. And don't make a mistake till the Stone is perfectly red ~ otherwise all is lost. Now praise God, and you can continue multiplying without end, always keeping one half out.

Finis.

www.ingramcontent.com/pod-product-compliance
Lightning Source LLC
Chambersburg PA
CBHW071808090426
42737CB00012B/1993